CROCK·POT®

◆ THE ORIGINAL SLOW COOKER ◆

SLOW COOKER
BIBLE

pil

Publications International, Ltd.

Photography on pages 25, 42, 45, 57, 59, 69, 74, 89, 113, 117, 156-163, 184, 204-217, 222, 248-253, 272, 286 and 289 by PIL Photo Studio
Photographer: Tate Hunt
Photographer's Assistant: Annemarie Zelasko Ruiz
Prop Stylist: Paula Walters
Food Stylists: Kim Hartman, Mary Ann Melone
Assistant Food Stylist: Michael Dueson

Pictured on the front cover: Middle Eastern-Spiced Beef, Tomatoes and Beans *(page 78)*.
Pictured on the back cover (clockwise from left): Northwest Beef and Vegetable Soup *(page 62)*, Forty-Clove Chicken *(page 131)* and Lemon Dilled Parsnips and Turnips *(page 256)*.

ISBN-13: 978-1-4508-0050-1
ISBN-10: 1-4508-0050-5

Library of Congress Control Number: 2010925365

Manufactured in China.

8 7 6 5 4 3 2 1

Table of Contents

The Joy of Slow Cooking

Slow Cooker Hints and Tips

Slow Cooker Sizes

Smaller slow cookers—such as 1- to 3½-quart models—are the perfect size for cooking for singles, a couple, or empty-nesters (and also for serving dips).

While medium-size slow cookers (those holding somewhere between 3 quarts and 5 quarts) will easily cook enough food at a time to feed a small family, they're also convenient for holiday side dishes or appetizers.

Large slow cookers are great for large family dinners, holiday entertaining, and potluck suppers. A 6-quart to 7-quart model is ideal if you like to make meals in advance, or have dinner tonight and store leftovers for another day.

Types of Slow Cookers

Current **CROCK-POT**® slow cookers come equipped with many different features and benefits, from auto cook programs to stovetop-safe stoneware to timed programming. Visit **www.crockpot.com** to find the slow cooker that best suits your needs.

How you plan to use a slow cooker may affect the model you choose to purchase. For everyday cooking, choose a size large enough to serve your family. If you plan to use the slow cooker primarily for entertaining, choose one of the larger sizes. Basic slow cookers can hold as little as 16 ounces or as much as 7 quarts. The smallest sizes are great for keeping dips hot on a buffet, while the larger sizes can more readily fit large quantities of food and larger roasts.

Cooking, Stirring, and Food Safety

CROCK-POT® slow cookers are safe to leave unattended. The outer heating base may get hot as it cooks, but it should not pose a fire hazard. The heating element in the heating base functions at a low wattage and is safe for your countertops.

Your slow cooker should be filled about one-half to three-fourths full for most recipes unless otherwise instructed. Lean meats such as chicken or pork tenderloin will cook faster than meats with more connective tissue and fat such as beef chuck or pork shoulder. Bone-in meats will take longer than boneless cuts. Typical slow cooker dishes take approximately 7 to 8 hours to reach the simmer point on LOW and about 3 to 4 hours on HIGH. Once the vegetables and meat start to simmer and braise, their flavors will fully blend and meat will become fall-off-the-bone tender.

According to the USDA, all bacteria are killed at a temperature of 165°F. It is important to follow the recommended cooking times and not to open the lid often, especially early in the cooking process when heat is building up inside the unit. If you need to open the lid to check on your food or are adding additional ingredients, remember to allow additional cooking time if necessary to ensure food is cooked through and tender.

Large slow cookers, the 6- to 7-quart sizes, may benefit with a quick stir halfway during cook time to help distribute heat and promote even cooking. It's usually unnecessary to stir at all, as even 1/2 cup liquid will help to distribute heat and the crockery is the perfect medium for holding food at an even temperature throughout the cooking process.

Oven-Safe

All **CROCK-POT®** slow cooker removable crockery inserts may (without their lids) be used safely in ovens at up to 400°F. Also, all **CROCK-POT®** slow cookers are microwavable without their lids. If you own another brand slow cooker, please refer to your owner's manual for specific crockery cooking medium tolerances.

Frozen Food

Frozen food or partially frozen food can be successfully cooked in a slow cooker; however, it will require longer cooking than the same recipe made with fresh food. It's almost always preferable to thaw frozen food prior to placing it in the slow cooker. Using an instant-read thermometer is recommended to ensure meat is fully cooked through.

Pasta and Rice

If you're converting a recipe that calls for uncooked pasta, cook the pasta on the stovetop just until slightly tender before adding to the slow cooker. If you are converting a recipe that calls for cooked rice, stir in raw rice with other ingredients; add 1/4 cup extra liquid per 1/4 cup of raw rice.

Beans

Beans must be softened completely before combining with sugar and/or acidic foods. Sugar and acid have a hardening effect on beans and will prevent softening. Fully cooked canned beans may be used as a substitute for dried beans.

Vegetables

Root vegetables often cook more slowly than meat. Cut vegetables accordingly to cook at the same rate as meat—large or small, or lean versus marbled—and place near the sides or bottom of the stoneware to facilitate cooking.

Herbs

Fresh herbs add flavor and color when added at the end of the cooking cycle; if added at the beginning, many fresh herbs' flavor will dissipate over long cook times. Ground and/or dried herbs and spices work well in slow cooking and may be added at the beginning, and for dishes with shorter cook times, hearty fresh herbs such as

rosemary and thyme hold up well. The flavor power of all herbs and spices can vary greatly depending on their particular strength and shelf life. Use chili powders and garlic powder sparingly, as these can sometimes intensify over the long cook times. Always taste dish at end of cook cycle and correct seasonings including salt and pepper.

Liquids

It is not necessary to use more than ½ to 1 cup liquid in most instances since juices in meats and vegetables are retained more in slow cooking than in conventional cooking. Excess liquid can be cooked down and concentrated after slow cooking on the stovetop or by

removing meat and vegetables from stoneware, stirring in one of the following thickeners, and setting the slow cooker to HIGH. Cook on HIGH for approximately 15 minutes until juices are thickened.

Flour: All-purpose flour is often used to thicken soups or stews. Place flour in a small bowl or cup and stir in enough cold water to make a thin, lump-free mixture. With the slow cooker on HIGH, quickly stir the flour mixture into the liquid in the slow cooker. Cook, stirring frequently, until the mixture thickens.

Cornstarch: Cornstarch gives sauces a clear, shiny appearance; it is used most often for sweet dessert sauces and stir-fry sauces. Place cornstarch in a small bowl or cup and stir in cold

water, stirring until the cornstarch dissolves. Quickly stir this mixture into the liquid in the slow cooker; the sauce will thicken as soon as the liquid boils. Cornstarch breaks down with too much heat, so never add it at the beginning of the slow cooking process, and turn off the heat as soon as the sauce thickens.

Arrowroot: Arrowroot (or arrowroot flour) comes from the root of a tropical plant that is dried and ground to a powder; it produces a thick clear sauce. Those who are allergic to wheat often use it in place of flour. Place arrowroot in a small bowl or cup and stir in cold water until the mixture is smooth. Quickly stir this mixture into the liquid in the slow cooker. Arrowroot thickens below the boiling point, so it even works well in a slow cooker on LOW. Too much stirring can break down an arrowroot mixture.

Tapioca: Tapioca is a starchy substance extracted from the root of the cassava plant. Its greatest advantage is that it withstands long cooking, making it an ideal choice for slow cooking. Add it at the beginning of cooking and you'll get a clear thickened sauce in the finished dish. Dishes using tapioca as a thickener are best cooked on the LOW setting; tapioca may become stringy when boiled for a long time.

Milk

Milk, cream, and sour cream break down during extended cooking. When possible, add during last 15 to 30 minutes of cooking, until just heated through. Condensed soups may be substituted for milk and can cook for extended times.

Fish

Fish is delicate and should be stirred in gently during the last 15 to 30 minutes of cooking time. Cook until just cooked through and serve immediately.

Baked Goods

If you wish to prepare bread, cakes, or pudding cakes in a slow cooker, you may want to purchase a covered, vented metal cake pan accessory for your slow cooker. You can also use any straight-sided soufflé dish or deep cake pan that will fit into the ceramic insert of your unit. Baked goods can be prepared directly in the insert; however they can be a little difficult to remove from the insert, so follow the recipe directions carefully.

Appetizers and Snacks

Thai Chicken Wings

1 tablespoon peanut oil

5 pounds chicken wings, tips removed and split at the joint

½ cup coconut milk

1 tablespoon Thai green curry paste

1 tablespoon fish sauce

1 tablespoon sugar

¾ cup prepared spicy peanut sauce

1. Heat oil in large nonstick skillet over medium-high heat. Add chicken wings and brown in several batches, about 6 minutes per batch. Transfer wings to **CROCK-POT®** slow cooker as they are browned.

2. Stir in coconut milk, curry paste, fish sauce and sugar. Cover and cook on LOW 6 to 7 hours or on HIGH 3 to 3½ hours or until tender. Drain cooking liquid and carefully stir in peanut sauce before serving.

Makes 8 servings

Chicken and Asiago Stuffed Mushrooms

20 large white mushrooms, stems removed and reserved

3 tablespoons extra-virgin olive oil, divided

¼ cup finely chopped onion

2 cloves garlic, minced

¼ cup Madeira wine

½ pound uncooked chicken sausage, removed from casings or ground chicken

1 cup grated Asiago cheese

¼ cup seasoned Italian bread crumbs

3 tablespoons chopped fresh parsley

½ teaspoon salt

¼ teaspoon black pepper

Tip: Stuffed mushrooms are a great way to impress guests with your gourmet home-cooking skills. These appetizers appear fancy and time-intensive, but they are actually simple with the help of a CROCK-POT® slow cooker.

1. Lightly brush mushroom caps with 1 tablespoon oil and set aside. Finely chop mushroom stems.

2. Heat remaining 2 tablespoons oil in large nonstick skillet over medium-high heat. Add onion and cook until just beginning to soften, about 1 minute. Add mushroom stems and cook until beginning to brown, 5 to 6 minutes. Stir in garlic and continue cooking 1 minute.

3. Pour in Madeira and cook until it evaporates, about 1 minute. Add sausage and cook, stirring to break into small pieces, until no longer pink, 3 to 4 minutes. Remove from heat and cool 5 minutes. Stir in cheese, bread crumbs, parsley, salt and pepper.

4. Divide mushroom-sausage mixture among mushroom caps, pressing slightly to compress. Place stuffed mushroom caps in single layer in **CROCK-POT®** slow cooker; cover and cook on LOW 4 hours or on HIGH 2 hours or until mushrooms are tender and filling is cooked through.

Makes 4 to 5 servings

Hot Broccoli Cheese Dip

½ cup (1 stick) butter

6 stalks celery, sliced

2 onions, chopped

2 cans (4 ounces each) sliced mushrooms, drained

¼ cup plus 2 tablespoons all-purpose flour

2 cans (10¾ ounces each) condensed cream of celery soup

5 to 6 ounces garlic cheese, cut into cubes

2 packages (10 ounces each) frozen broccoli spears

French bread slices, bell pepper strips, cherry tomatoes

1. Melt butter in large skillet. Add celery, onions and mushrooms; cook and stir until translucent. Stir in flour and cook 2 to 3 minutes. Transfer to **CROCK-POT**® slow cooker.

2. Stir in soup, cheese and broccoli. Cover; cook on HIGH, stirring every 15 minutes, until cheese is melted. Turn **CROCK-POT**® slow cooker to LOW. Cover; cook 2 to 4 hours or until ready to serve.

3. Serve warm with bread slices and assorted vegetables.

Makes about 6 cups

Asian Barbecue Skewers

2 **pounds boneless, skinless
chicken thighs**

½ **cup soy sauce**

⅓ **cup packed brown sugar**

2 **tablespoons sesame oil**

3 **cloves garlic, minced**

½ **cup thinly sliced scallions**

1 **tablespoon toasted
sesame seeds (optional)**

1. Cut each thigh into 4 pieces about 1½ inches thick. Thread chicken onto 7-inch-long wooden skewers, folding thinner pieces, if necessary. Place skewers into **CROCK-POT**® slow cooker, layering as flat as possible.

2. Combine soy sauce, brown sugar, oil and garlic in small bowl. Reserve ⅓ cup sauce; set aside. Pour remaining sauce over skewers. Cover; cook on LOW 2 hours. Turn skewers over and cook 1 hour longer.

3. Transfer skewers to serving platter. Discard cooking liquid. Spoon on reserved sauce and sprinkle with sliced scallions and sesame seeds, if desired.

Makes 4 to 6 servings

Curried Snack Mix

3 **tablespoons butter**

2 **tablespoons packed light
brown sugar**

1½ **teaspoons hot curry
powder**

¼ **teaspoon salt**

¼ **teaspoon ground cumin**

2 **cups rice cereal squares**

1 **cup walnut halves**

1 **cup dried cranberries**

Melt butter in large skillet. Add brown sugar, curry powder, salt and cumin; mix well. Add cereal, walnuts and cranberries; stir to coat. Transfer mixture to **CROCK-POT**® slow cooker. Cover; cook on LOW 3 hours. Remove cover; cook, uncovered, 30 minutes.

Makes 16 servings

Asian Barbeque Skewers

Chicken Liver Pâté

Pâté

1½ **pounds chicken livers, trimmed of fat and membrane**

1 **small onion, thinly sliced**

3 **sprigs fresh thyme**

2 **cloves garlic, peeled and smashed**

¼ **teaspoon salt**

1 **tablespoon water**

3 **tablespoons cold butter, cut into 4 pieces**

2 **tablespoons heavy cream**

2 **tablespoons sherry**

Garnish

½ **shallot, minced (optional)**

2 **tablespoons chopped fresh parsley (optional)**

1 **tablespoon sherry vinegar (optional)**

⅛ **teaspoon sugar**

Salt and black pepper to taste

Melba toast or toast points

1. Rinse chicken livers and pat dry. Place in **CROCK-POT®** slow cooker. Add onion, thyme, garlic, salt and water. Cover and cook on LOW 2 hours.

2. Remove thyme sprigs from cooked livers and discard. Pour remaining ingredients from **CROCK-POT®** slow cooker into strainer and cool until just warm to the touch. Transfer to food processor and pulse just long enough to coarsely chop livers. Add butter, one piece at a time, pulsing just enough after each addition to combine butter with liver pâté.

3. Add heavy cream and sherry and pulse once or twice more to combine. Transfer to serving bowl and serve immediately. Alternatively, transfer to a small loaf pan, pressing plastic wrap to surface of pâté. Refrigerate overnight, tightly wrapped in additional plastic wrap. Unmold pâté and slice to serve.

4. To garnish pâté (room temperature or refrigerated), stir together shallot, if desired, parsley, vinegar, sugar, salt and pepper in small bowl. Set aside 5 minutes, then spoon over pâté. Serve with Melba toast or toast points.

Makes 8 to 10 servings

Creamy Seafood Dip

1 package (8 ounces) pepper jack cheese, shredded

1 can (6 ounces) lump crabmeat, drained

1 pound cooked shrimp, peeled, deveined and chopped

1 cup heavy whipping cream, divided

1 round sourdough bread loaf (about 1 pound)

1. Place cheese in **CROCK-POT®** slow cooker, and turn to HIGH. Add crabmeat, shrimp and ³/₄ cup cream. Stir well to combine. Cover; cook 10 to 15 minutes or until cheese is melted.

2. Meanwhile, cut off top of bread and hollow out to create bowl. Cut extra bread into large pieces. Place bread bowl on serving plate. Place extra bread around bowl.

3. Check consistency of dip. Stir in up to ¹/₄ cup additional cream, as needed. To serve, pour into bread bowl.

Makes 6 to 8 servings

Party Mix

3 cups bite-size rice cereal squares

2 cups toasted oat ring cereal

2 cups bite-size wheat cereal squares

1 cup peanuts or pistachio nuts

1 cup thin pretzel sticks

¹/₂ cup (1 stick) butter, melted

1 tablespoon Worcestershire sauce

1 teaspoon seasoned salt

¹/₂ teaspoon garlic powder

¹/₈ teaspoon ground red pepper (optional)

1. Combine cereals, nuts and pretzels in **CROCK-POT®** slow cooker.

2. Mix butter, Worcestershire sauce, seasoned salt, garlic powder and red pepper, if desired, in small bowl. Pour over cereal mixture in **CROCK-POT®** slow cooker; toss lightly to coat.

3. Cover; cook on LOW 3 hours, stirring well every 30 minutes. Cook, uncovered, 30 minutes more. Store cooled Party Mix in airtight container.

Makes 10 cups

Creamy Seafood Dip

Caponata

1   **medium eggplant (about
    1 pound), peeled and cut
    into ¹/₂-inch pieces**

1   **can (14¹/₂ ounces) diced
    Italian plum tomatoes,
    undrained**

1   **medium onion, chopped**

1   **red bell pepper, cut into
    ¹/₂-inch pieces**

¹/₂ **cup medium-hot salsa**

¹/₄ **cup extra-virgin olive oil**

2   **tablespoons capers,
    drained**

2   **tablespoons balsamic
    vinegar**

3   **cloves garlic, minced**

1   **teaspoon dried oregano**

¹/₄ **teaspoon salt**

¹/₃ **cup packed fresh basil,
    cut into thin strips**

    **Toasted sliced Italian
    or French bread**

1. Mix eggplant, tomatoes with juice, onion, bell pepper, salsa, oil, capers, vinegar, garlic, oregano and salt in **CROCK-POT®** slow cooker.

2. Cover; cook on LOW 7 to 8 hours or until vegetables are crisp-tender.

3. Stir in basil. Serve at room temperature with toasted bread.

Makes about 5¹/₄ cups

Tropical Chicken Wings

3 **pounds chicken wings cut apart at joint, wing tips removed and discarded**
1 **jar (12 ounces) pineapple preserves**
½ **cup soy sauce**
½ **cup chopped green onions**
3 **tablespoons fresh lime juice**
2 **tablespoons pomegranate molasses or honey**
1 **tablespoon minced garlic**
2 **teaspoons sriracha sauce***
¼ **teaspoon ground allspice**
1 **tablespoon toasted sesame seed**

*Sriracha is a spicy chili sauce made from dried chiles and used as a condiment in several Asian cuisines. It can be found in the ethnic section of major supermarkets, but an equal amount of hot pepper sauce may be substituted.

Tip: Pomegranate molasses is a syrup made from pomegranate juice cooked with sugar. You can easily make your own if it isn't in the ethnic foods aisle of your local supermarket. For this recipe, bring to a boil ½ cup pomegranate juice, 2 tablespoons sugar and 1 teaspoon lemon juice in a small sauce pan over medium-high heat. Cook, stirring occasionally, until reduced to about 2 tablespoons. Use as directed above.

1. Cut chicken wings apart at the joint. Remove and discard Place the chicken wings in **CROCK-POT®** slow cooker.

2. Combine preserves, soy sauce, green onions, lime juice, pomegranate molasses, garlic, sriracha sauce and allspice in small bowl. Pour over wings.

3. Cover and cook on LOW 3 to 4 hours or until wings are fork tender.

4. Sprinkle with sesame seeds just before serving.

Makes 6 to 8 servings

Sausage and Swiss Chard Stuffed Mushrooms

2 packages (6 ounces each) baby portobello mushrooms or large brown stuffing mushrooms*

4 tablespoons extra-virgin olive oil, divided

½ teaspoon salt, divided

½ teaspoon black pepper, divided

½ pound bulk pork sausage

½ onion, finely chopped

2 cups chopped Swiss chard, rinsed

¼ teaspoon dried thyme

2 tablespoons garlic-and-herb-flavored dried bread crumbs

1½ cups chicken broth, divided

2 tablespoons grated Parmesan cheese

2 tablespoons chopped fresh parsley

*Use "baby bellas" or cremini mushrooms. Do not substitute white button mushrooms.

Variation: If desired, place a small square of sliced Swiss cheese on each mushroom and continue cooking 15 minutes longer or until cheese is melted. Proceed as directed.

1. Coat **CROCK-POT**® slow cooker with nonstick cooking spray. Wipe mushrooms clean, remove stems and hollow out mushroom caps. Pour 3 tablespoons oil into small bowl. Brush mushrooms inside and out with oil. Season mushrooms with ¼ teaspoon salt and ¼ teaspoon pepper; set aside.

2. Heat remaining 1 tablespoon oil in medium skillet over medium heat until hot. Add sausage. Cook and stir until browned. Transfer sausage with slotted spoon to medium bowl.

3. Add onion to skillet. Cook and stir, loosening browned bits, about 3 minutes or until translucent. Stir in chard and thyme. Cook until chard is just wilted, about 1 to 2 minutes.

4. Remove skillet from heat. Add sausage, bread crumbs, 1 tablespoon broth, remaining ¼ teaspoon salt and remaining ¼ teaspoon pepper. Mix well to combine. Scoop 1 tablespoon stuffing into each mushroom cap. Divide remaining stuffing evenly among mushrooms.

5. Pour remaining broth into **CROCK-POT**® slow cooker. Arrange stuffed mushrooms in bottom. Cover; cook on HIGH 3 hours or until mushrooms are tender. To serve, remove mushrooms with slotted spoon; discard cooking liquid. Blend cheese and parsley and sprinkle onto mushrooms.

Makes 6 to 8 servings

Warm Moroccan-Style Bean Dip

2 teaspoons canola oil

1 small onion, chopped

2 cloves garlic, minced

2 cans (15 ounces each) cannellini beans, rinsed and drained

¾ cup canned diced tomatoes, drained

½ teaspoon ground turmeric (optional)

¼ teaspoon ground cinnamon

¼ teaspoon paprika

¼ teaspoon black pepper

¼ teaspoon salt

¼ teaspoon ground cumin

⅛ teaspoon ground cloves

⅛ teaspoon ground red pepper

2 tablespoons plain yogurt

1 tablespoon cool water

¼ teaspoon dried mint (optional)

Warm pita bread, cut into wedges

Tip: Moroccan cuisine has a wide array of dishes beyond the most famous couscous. The cuisine makes use of a wide variety of spices; this reflects the many ethnicities that have influenced the country over the centuries. This spice-filled dip is sure to stimulate guests' taste buds and conversation with its combination of exotic flavors.

1. Heat oil in small skillet over medium-high heat. Add onion and cook until translucent (5 to 6 minutes). Add garlic and cook 45 seconds more. Transfer to **CROCK-POT**® slow cooker. Stir in beans, tomatoes and spices. Cover and cook on LOW 6 hours.

2. Transfer bean mixture and cooking liquid to food processor or blender and pulse to make coarse paste. Alternatively, use immersion blender to chop beans to coarse paste in **CROCK-POT**® slow cooker. Transfer to serving plate or bowl.

3. Beat yogurt and cold water together until well combined. Drizzle over bean dip and garnish with dried mint, if desired. Serve warm with pita bread wedges for dipping.

Makes 4 to 6 servings

Bagna Cauda

¾ **cup olive oil**

6 **tablespoons butter, softened**

12 **anchovy fillets, drained**

6 **cloves garlic, peeled**

⅛ **teaspoon red pepper flakes**

Assorted foods for dipping such as endive spears, cauliflower florettes, cucumber spears, carrot sticks, zucchini spears, red bell pepper pieces, sugar snap peas or crusty Italian or French bread slices

---

Tip: Bagna cauda is a warm Italian dip similar to the more famous fondue. The name is derived from "bagno caldo," meaning "warm bath" in Italian. This dip should be kept warm while serving, just like you would fondue.

Place olive oil, butter, anchovies, garlic and red pepper flakes in food processor and process until quite smooth, about 30 seconds. Scrape mixture into 2½-quart **CROCK-POT**® slow cooker. Cover and cook on LOW 2 hours or on HIGH 1 hour or until mixture is hot. Turn to LOW and serve with assorted dippers.

Makes 10 to 12 servings

Party Meatballs

1 **package (about 1 pound)
   frozen cocktail-size
   turkey or beef meatballs**

½ **cup maple syrup**

1 **jar (12 ounces) chili sauce**

1 **jar (12 ounces) grape jelly**

Place meatballs, syrup, chili sauce and jelly in **CROCK-POT®** slow cooker. Stir to combine. Cover and cook on LOW 3 to 4 hours or on HIGH 2 to 3 hours. Serve warm.

Makes 10 to 12 servings

Warm Blue Crab Bruschetta

**4 cups peeled, seeded
and diced Roma or plum
tomatoes**

1 cup diced white onion

2 teaspoons minced garlic

1/3 cup olive oil

**2 tablespoons balsamic
vinegar**

1/2 teaspoon dried oregano

2 tablespoons sugar

**1 pound lump blue
crabmeat, picked over
for shells**

1 1/2 teaspoons kosher salt

**1/2 teaspoon cracked black
pepper**

1/3 cup minced fresh basil

**2 baguettes, sliced and
toasted**

**Serving Suggestion: Crab
topping can also be served
on Melba toast or whole-
grain crackers.**

1. Combine tomatoes, onion, garlic, oil, vinegar, oregano and sugar in **CROCK-POT®** slow cooker. Cover; cook on LOW 2 hours.

2. Add crabmeat, salt and pepper. Stir gently to mix, taking care not to break up crabmeat lumps. Cook on LOW 1 hour.

3. Fold in basil. Serve on toasted baguette slices.

Makes 16 servings

Pizza Fondue

½ **pound bulk Italian sausage**

1 **cup chopped onion**

2 **jars (26 ounces each) meatless pasta sauce**

4 **ounces thinly sliced ham, finely chopped**

1 **package (3 ounces) sliced pepperoni, finely chopped**

¼ **teaspoon red pepper flakes**

1 **pound mozzarella cheese, cut into ¾-inch cubes**

1 **loaf Italian or French bread, cut into 1-inch cubes**

1. Cook and stir sausage and onion in large skillet over medium-high heat until sausage is browned Drain and discard fat.

2. Transfer sausage mixture to **CROCK-POT**® slow cooker. Stir in pasta sauce, ham, pepperoni and red pepper flakes. Cover; cook on LOW 3 to 4 hours. Serve warm fondue with mozzarella cheese and bread cubes.

Makes 20 to 25 appetizer servings

Creamy Cheesy Spinach Dip

2 packages (10 ounces each) frozen chopped spinach, thawed

2 cups chopped onions

1 teaspoon salt

1/2 teaspoon garlic powder

1/4 teaspoon black pepper

12 ounces pasteurized processed cheese spread with jalapeño peppers, cubed

Cherry tomatoes with pulp removed (optional)

Sliced cucumbers (optional)

Assorted crackers (optional)

Tip: To thaw spinach quickly, remove paper wrapper from spinach containers. Microwave on HIGH (100% power) 3 to 4 minutes or until just thawed.

1. Drain spinach and squeeze dry, reserving 3/4 cup liquid. Place spinach, reserved liquid, onions, salt, garlic powder and pepper into 1 1/2-quart or other small-sized **CROCK-POT**® slow cooker; stir to blend. Cover; cook on HIGH 1 1/2 hours.

2. Stir in cheese and cook 30 minutes longer or until melted. Fill cherry tomato shells, spread on cucumber slices or serve with crackers, if desired.

Makes about 4 cups

Tomato Topping for Bruschetta

6 **medium tomatoes,
peeled, cored, seeded and
diced**

2 **celery stalks, trimmed
and chopped**

2 **shallots, chopped**

4 **pepperoncini peppers,
chopped***

2 **teaspoons tomato paste**

1 **teaspoon salt**

1/2 **teaspoon black pepper**

2 **tablespoons olive oil**

8 **slices country bread or
other large round bread**

2 **cloves garlic**

*Pepperoncini are pickled peppers
sold in jars with brine. They're
available in the supermarket
condiment aisle.

**Variation: To serve as a
main dish, omit bread and
garlic, and toss tomato
topping with cooked penne
pasta. You may also spoon
the topping over roasted
chicken breasts as a
flavorful sauce.**

1. Drain off any tomato juices. Combine tomatoes, celery,
shallots, pepperoncini peppers, tomato paste, salt, black pepper
and oil in **CROCK-POT**® slow cooker. Cover; cook on LOW
45 minutes to 1 hour.

2. Toast bread. Immediately rub with garlic. Spread tomato
topping on bread. Serve immediately.

Makes 8 servings

Cocktail Meatballs

- **1 pound 95% lean ground beef**
- **1 pound bulk pork or Italian sausage**
- **1 cup cracker crumbs**
- **1 cup finely chopped onion**
- **1 cup finely chopped green bell pepper**
- **½ cup milk**
- **1 egg, beaten**
- **2 teaspoons salt**
- **1 teaspoon dried Italian seasoning**
- **¼ teaspoon black pepper**
- **1 cup ketchup**
- **¾ cup packed dark brown sugar**
- **½ cup (1 stick) butter or margarine**
- **½ cup vinegar**
- **¼ cup lemon juice**
- **¼ cup water**
- **1 teaspoon prepared mustard**
- **¼ teaspoon garlic salt**

1. Preheat oven to 350°F. Combine beef, pork, cracker crumbs, onion, bell pepper, milk, egg, salt, Italian seasoning and black pepper in bowl. Mix well; form into 1-inch meatballs. Place meatballs onto 2 nonstick baking sheets. Bake 25 minutes or until browned.

2. Meanwhile, place ketchup, sugar, butter, vinegar, lemon juice, water, mustard and garlic salt into **CROCK-POT®** slow cooker; mix well. Cover; cook on HIGH 15 to 20 minutes or until hot.

3. Transfer meatballs to **CROCK-POT®** slow cooker; carefully stir to coat with sauce. Reduce heat to LOW. Cover; cook 2 hours.

Makes about 24 meatballs

Chorizo and Queso Fundido

2 **cured chorizo sausages
(about 3½ ounces total),
finely chopped***

8 **ounces Monterey Jack
cheese, cubed**

8 **ounces cream cheese,
cubed**

8 **ounces processed cheese
spread, cubed**

8 **ounces Cheddar cheese,
cubed**

1 **tablespoon
Worcestershire sauce**

Tortilla chips

*There are two styles of chorizo
widely available in most major
supermarkets. Mexican-style, or
uncured, chorizo is typically sold
in ½- or 1-pound refrigerated
packages. Spanish-style, or cured,
chorizo is sold in links of varying
sizes held together by their casings.

**Tip: In Spanish, queso
fundido means "melted
cheese", which precisely
describes this dish. For
a more authentic taste,
replace some of the cheeses
with Mexican cheeses such
as queso fresco, chihuahua
or cotija.**

Combine chorizo, cheeses and Worcestershire sauce in
CROCK-POT® slow cooker. Cover and cook on HIGH 1 to
1½ hours or until cheese looks very soft; whisk to blend and
keep warm on LOW or WARM. Serve with tortilla chips.

Makes 8 to 12 servings

Honey-Mustard Chicken Wings

3 pounds chicken wings

1 teaspoon salt

1 teaspoon black pepper

½ cup honey

½ cup barbecue sauce

**2 tablespoons spicy brown
mustard**

1 clove garlic, minced

3 to 4 thin lemon slices

1. Preheat broiler. Cut off wing tips; discard. Cut each wing at joint to make 2 pieces. Season with salt and pepper. Place on broiler pan. Broil 4 to 5 inches from heat about 5 minutes per side. Transfer to **CROCK-POT**® slow cooker.

2. Combine honey, barbecue sauce, mustard and garlic in small bowl; mix well. Pour sauce over chicken wings. Top with lemon slices. Cover; cook on LOW 4 to 5 hours. Before serving, remove and discard lemon slices. Serve wings with sauce.

Makes 4 to 5 appetizer servings

Firecracker Black Bean Dip

1 **can (16 ounces) refried black beans**

¾ **cup prepared salsa**

1 **poblano pepper or 2 jalapeño peppers, seeded and minced***

1 **teaspoon chili powder**

½ **cup crumbled queso fresco****

3 **green onions, sliced**

Tortilla chips

Assorted cut-up vegetables

*Jalapeño peppers can sting and irritate the skin, so wear rubber gloves when handling peppers and do not touch your eyes.

**Queso fresco is a mild white Mexican cheese. If unavailable, substitute shredded Monterey Jack or Cheddar cheese.

1. Combine beans, salsa, pepper and chili powder in 2-quart **CROCK-POT®** slow cooker. Cover; cook on LOW 3 to 4 hours or on HIGH 2 hours.

2. Top with cheese and green onions. Serve warm with tortilla chips and vegetables.

Makes 8 to 10 servings

Thai Coconut Chicken Meatballs

1 **pound ground chicken**

2 **green onions (white and green parts), chopped**

1 **clove garlic, minced**

2 **teaspoons toasted sesame oil**

1 **teaspoon fish sauce**

2 **teaspoons mirin (Japanese sweet rice wine)**

1 **tablespoon canola oil**

1/2 **cup unsweetened canned coconut milk**

1/4 **cup chicken broth**

1 **teaspoon Thai red curry paste**

2 **teaspoons packed brown sugar**

2 **teaspoons lime juice**

1 **tablespoon cornstarch**

2 **tablespoons cold water**

Tip: Meatballs that are of equal size will cook at the same rate and be done at the same time. To ensure your meatballs are the same size, pat seasoned ground meat into an even rectangle and then slice into even rows and columns. Roll each portion into smooth ball.

1. Combine chicken, green onions, garlic, sesame oil, fish sauce and mirin in large bowl. Mix well to combine and shape into meatballs about 1½ inches in diameter.

2. Heat canola oil in large skillet over medium-high heat. Add meatballs and cook, rolling to brown on all sides. Transfer to **CROCK-POT**® slow cooker. Add coconut milk, chicken broth, curry paste and sugar. Cover and cook on HIGH 3½ to 4 hours. Stir in lime juice.

3. Stir cornstarch into cold water, mixing until smooth. Stir in additional water as needed to reach consistency of heavy cream. Stir into sauce in **CROCK-POT**® slow cooker. Cook uncovered 10 to 15 minutes until sauce is slightly thickened and evenly coats meatballs.

Makes 4 to 5 servings

Spicy Sweet & Sour Cocktail Franks

2 packages (8 ounces each) cocktail franks

½ cup ketchup or chili sauce

½ cup apricot preserves

1 teaspoon hot pepper sauce

Additional hot pepper sauce (optional)

1. Combine all ingredients in 1½-quart **CROCK-POT®** slow cooker; mix well. Cover; cook on LOW 2 to 3 hours.

2. Serve warm or at room temperature with additional hot pepper sauce, if desired.

Makes about 4 dozen

Soups, Stews and Chilies

Black Bean and Turkey Stew

3 cans (15 ounces each) black beans, rinsed and drained

1½ cups chopped onions

1½ cups fat-free reduced-sodium chicken broth

1 cup sliced celery

1 cup chopped red bell pepper

4 cloves garlic, minced

1½ teaspoons dried oregano leaves

¾ teaspoon ground coriander

½ teaspoon ground cumin

¼ teaspoon ground red pepper

6 ounces cooked turkey sausage, thinly sliced

1. Combine all ingredients except sausage in **CROCK-POT®** slow cooker. Cover; cook on LOW 6 to 8 hours.

2. Transfer about 1½ cups bean mixture from **CROCK-POT®** slow cooker to blender or food processor; purée bean mixture. Return to **CROCK-POT®** slow cooker. Stir in sausage. Cover; cook on LOW an additional 10 to 15 minutes.

Makes 6 servings

Tuscan Beef Stew

½ **cup hot beef broth**

¼ **cup dried porcini mushrooms**

3 **slices bacon, diced**

1 **tablespoon olive oil**

2 **pounds lean stew beef**

Salt

Black pepper

3 **cups assorted fresh mushrooms (such as Portobello, shiitake or cremini)**

1 **cup frozen pearl onions, thawed**

1 **cup baby carrots cut into ½-inch pieces**

1 **cup dry red wine**

1 **can (15 ounces) diced tomatoes with roasted garlic, undrained**

¼ **cup tomato paste**

1 **tablespoon chopped fresh rosemary or 1 teaspoon dried rosemary**

½ **teaspoon sugar**

2 **tablespoons all-purpose flour**

2 **tablespoons butter, softened**

Hot cooked pasta

1. Combine hot beef broth and dried porcini mushrooms in a small bowl. Let stand until softened. Remove mushrooms and chop coarsely. Reserve broth.

2. Cook bacon in a large skillet over medium-high heat until crisp. Transfer with slotted spoon to paper towels to drain. Pour off bacon drippings from skillet. Add olive oil to pan. Season beef with salt and pepper and cook over medium-high heat until browned on all sides. Place in **CROCK-POT®** slow cooker.

3. Add bacon, chopped porcini mushrooms, fresh mushrooms, onions, carrots, wine, tomatoes with juice, tomato paste, rosemary and sugar. Carefully pour reserved beef broth over other ingredients, being sure to keep sediment in bottom of bowl. Cover and cook on LOW 7 to 8 hours until beef is fork-tender.

4. Combine flour and butter in a small bowl and mash into smooth paste. Stir half of paste into cooking liquid. Cover and cook 15 minutes. If thicker gravy is desired, repeat with remaining flour paste. Serve over pasta.

Makes 6 to 8 servings

Chicken Miso Soup with Shiitake Mushrooms

16 chicken thighs (about 5 pounds) with skin and bone

3 to 4 cups chicken stock

3 tablespoons canola oil

2 large onions, coarsely chopped

1 pound fresh shiitake mushrooms, stems discarded, large caps quartered

3 tablespoons finely chopped peeled ginger

3 tablespoons finely chopped garlic

1 cup mirin (Japanese sweet rice wine)

1 cup white miso paste

½ cup soy sauce

4 cups water

1 pound (about 16 cups) mustard greens, tough stems and ribs discarded and leaves coarsely chopped

Cooked white rice (optional)

Thinly sliced green onions, for garnish

1. Preheat oven to 500°F with rack in middle.

2. Pat chicken dry, then roast, skin side up, in 1 layer on 17 × 12-inch rimmed sheet pan or jelly-roll pan with sides until skin is golden brown, 35 to 40 minutes.

3. Transfer roasted chicken and pan liquids to large measure and spoon off any fat that rises to surface. Add enough stock to bring liquid to 4 cups total.

4. Heat oil in skillet over medium heat and sauté onions until softened and beginning to brown. Add mushrooms, ginger and garlic, and sauté until garlic is golden, 3 to 5 minutes.

5. Add mirin to pan and bring to a boil, stirring and scraping up any brown bits for 1 minute. Pour into **CROCK-POT**® slow cooker. Stir in miso paste and soy sauce, then add chicken, stock mixture and water. Cover and cook on LOW 8 to 9 hours or on HIGH 4 to 5 hours or until chicken is tender.

6. Stir in mustard greens and continue to cook, covered, 5 minutes or until greens are wilted. Taste and adjust seasonings as desired. Serve in shallow bowls with cooked white rice, if desired, and garnish with green onions.

Makes 6 to 8 servings

Soupe au Pistou

2 tablespoons olive oil

¼ pound pancetta, chopped

2 onions, chopped

2 cloves garlic, mashed

2 leeks, chopped

½ pound small zucchini, diced

1 can (15 ounces) lima beans, drained and rinsed

1 can (14 ounces) diced plum tomatoes, drained or 3 to 4 fresh plum tomatoes, chopped

6 to 8 cups chicken stock

½ pound fresh green beans, cut into 1½-inch pieces

2 cans (15 ounces each) cannellini beans, drained and rinsed

½ pound small pasta, such as ditalini, cooked al dente

Salt and black pepper

½ cup Parmesan cheese, grated

6 tablespoons butter

3 cloves garlic, minced

2 bunches fresh basil leaves, chopped

Serving Suggestion: Serve with crusty French bread.

1. Heat oil in skillet over medium heat. Add pancetta, onions, garlic and leeks and cook, stirring, until softened. Transfer mixture to **CROCK-POT®** slow cooker.

2. Add zucchini, lima beans, tomatoes and enough stock to cover vegetables. Cover and cook on LOW 6 to 7 hours or on HIGH 3½ hours.

3. Add green beans, cannellini beans and pasta. Cover and cook an additional 15 minutes on HIGH or until green beans are crisp-tender and bright green. Season to taste with salt and pepper.

4. For garnish, combine Parmesan, butter, garlic and basil in food processor. Use on/off pulses to make coarse paste. Ladle soup into individual bowls and garnish with Parmesan mixture.

Makes 6 to 8 servings

Chinese Chicken Stew

1 **pound boneless, skinless chicken thighs, cut into 1-inch pieces**

1 **teaspoon Chinese five-spice powder***

½ **to ¾ teaspoon red pepper flakes**

1 **tablespoon peanut or vegetable oil**

1 **large onion, coarsely chopped**

1 **package (8 ounces) fresh mushrooms, sliced**

2 **cloves garlic, minced**

1 **can (about 14 ounces) chicken broth, divided**

1 **tablespoon cornstarch**

1 **large red bell pepper, cut into ¾-inch pieces**

2 **tablespoons soy sauce**

2 **large green onions, cut into ½-inch pieces**

1 **tablespoon sesame oil**

3 **cups hot cooked white rice (optional)**

¼ **cup coarsely chopped fresh cilantro (optional)**

*Chinese five-spice powder is a blend of cinnamon, cloves, fennel seed, anise and Szechuan peppercorns. It is available in most supermarkets and at Asian grocery stores.

1. Toss chicken with five-spice powder and red pepper flakes in small bowl. Heat peanut oil in large skillet. Add onion and chicken; cook and stir about 5 minutes or until chicken is browned. Add mushrooms and garlic; cook and stir until chicken is no longer pink.

2. Combine ¼ cup broth and cornstarch in small bowl; set aside. Place cooked chicken mixture, remaining broth, bell pepper and soy sauce in **CROCK-POT**® slow cooker. Cover; cook on LOW 3½ hours or until peppers are tender.

3. Stir in cornstarch mixture, green onions and sesame oil. Cook 30 to 45 minutes or until thickened. Ladle into soup bowls; scoop ½ cup rice into each bowl and sprinkle with cilantro, if desired.

Makes 6 servings (about 5 cups)

Thai-Style Chicken Pumpkin Soup

1 tablespoon extra-virgin olive oil

6 boneless, skinless chicken breasts, cut into 1-inch cubes

1 large white onion, thinly sliced

3 cloves garlic, minced

1 tablespoon minced fresh ginger

½ to ¾ teaspoon crushed red pepper flakes

2 stalks celery, trimmed and diced

2 carrots, peeled, trimmed and diced

1 can (15 ounces) solid-pack pumpkin*

½ cup creamy peanut butter

4 cups low-sodium chicken broth

½ cup mango nectar

½ cup fresh lime juice

3 tablespoons rice vinegar

½ cup minced fresh cilantro, divided

½ cup heavy cream

1 tablespoon cornstarch

2 to 4 cups hot cooked rice (preferably jasmine or basmati)

3 green onions, minced

½ cup roasted unsalted peanuts, coarsely chopped

Lime wedges (optional)

*Not pumpkin pie filling.

1. Heat oil in large skillet over medium heat. Add chicken and cook, stirring occasionally, about 3 minutes. Add onion, garlic, ginger and red pepper flakes; cook for 1 or 2 minutes longer or until fragrant. Transfer chicken mixture to **CROCK-POT**® slow cooker.

2. Stir in celery, carrots, pumpkin, peanut butter, broth, mango nectar and lime juice. Cover; cook on LOW 8 hours or on HIGH 4 hours.

3. Stir in rice vinegar and ¼ cup cilantro. Stir together cream and cornstarch in small bowl. Stir into soup. Turn to HIGH. Simmer, uncovered, 10 minutes or until soup thickens.

4. To serve, put rice in soup bowls. Ladle soup around rice. Sprinkle with remaining cilantro, green onions and peanuts. Squeeze fresh lime juice over soup, if desired.

Makes 4 to 6 servings

Jerk Pork and Sweet Potato Stew

2 tablespoons all-purpose
flour

1/4 teaspoon salt, or to taste

1/4 teaspoon black pepper,
or to taste

1 1/4 pounds pork shoulder,
cut into bite-size pieces

2 tablespoons vegetable oil

1 large sweet potato,
peeled and diced

1 cup frozen or canned corn

1/4 cup minced green onions
(green parts only), divided

1 clove garlic, minced

1/2 medium scotch bonnet
chile or jalapeño pepper,
cored, seeded and minced
(about 1 teaspoon)*

1/8 teaspoon ground allspice

1 cup chicken broth

1 tablespoon lime juice

2 cups cooked rice
(optional)

*Scotch bonnet chiles and jalapeño
peppers can sting and irritate the
skin, so wear rubber gloves when
handling and do not touch your
eyes.

Tip: To reduce the amount
of fat in **CROCK-POT**® slow
cooker meals, trim excess
fat from meats and degrease
canned broth before using.

1. Combine flour, salt and pepper in resealable plastic food storage bag. Add pork and shake well to coat. Heat oil in large skillet over medium heat until hot. Add pork in a single layer (working in 2 batches, if necessary) and brown on both sides, about 5 minutes. Transfer to **CROCK-POT**® slow cooker.

2. Add sweet potato, corn, 2 tablespoons green onions, garlic, chile and allspice. Stir in broth. Cover; cook on LOW 5 to 6 hours.

3. Stir in lime juice and remaining 2 tablespoons green onions. Adjust salt and pepper to taste. Serve stew over cooked rice, if desired.

Makes 4 servings

Lentil and Portobello Soup

2 portobello mushrooms
(about 8 ounces total),
cleaned and trimmed

1 tablespoon olive oil

1 medium onion, chopped

2 medium carrots, cut into
1/2-inch-thick rounds

2 cloves garlic, minced

1 cup dried lentils

1 can (28 ounces) diced
tomatoes in juice,
undrained

1 can (14 1/2 ounces)
vegetable broth

1 teaspoon dried rosemary

1 bay leaf

Salt

Black pepper

1. Remove stems from mushrooms; coarsely chop stems. Cut each cap in half, then cut each half into 1/2-inch pieces. Set aside.

2. Heat oil in large skillet over medium heat. Add onion, carrots and garlic and cook, stirring occasionally, until onion softens. Transfer to **CROCK-POT**® slow cooker. Layer lentils, tomatoes with juice, vegetable broth, mushrooms caps and stems, dried rosemary and bay leaf on top of carrots and onion. Cover; cook on HIGH 5 to 6 hours or until lentils are tender. Remove bay leaf and season to taste with salt and pepper before serving. Serve hot.

Makes 6 servings

Slow Cooker Chicken Stock

1 large chicken (4 to
6 pounds), cut into pieces

1 package (16 ounces)
celery, cut into large
pieces

1 large carrot, peeled and
cut into 2- to 3-inch pieces

2 onions or leeks, quartered

2 large parsnips, peeled and
coarsely chopped

1/2 cup loosely packed fresh
herbs such as flat-leaf
parsley, dill, thyme,
chervil or a combination

Kosher salt and black
pepper, to taste

1. Place all ingredients in **CROCK-POT**® slow cooker and add enough water to fill three-quarters full. Cook 12 hours on LOW or 8 hours on HIGH.

2. Strain out solids, cool and refrigerate 12 hours. Skim off and discard any fat on top of stock.

Makes about 10 cups stock

Lentil and Portobello Soup

Beef Barley Soup

1½ **pounds lean beef stew meat, cut in ½-inch pieces**

1 **teaspoon salt**

½ **teaspoon black pepper**

2 **medium carrots, quartered lengthwise and cut into ½-inch pieces**

1 **cup chopped onion**

1 **package (8 ounces) sliced mushrooms**

1 **leek (white and pale green parts), halved and thinly sliced**

2 **tablespoons Worcestershire sauce**

1 **teaspoon soy sauce**

1 **bay leaf**

5 **cups beef broth**

1 **cup frozen mixed vegetables, thawed**

¾ **cup medium barley**

1. Season beef with salt and pepper and place in **CROCK-POT®** slow cooker. Add carrots, onion, mushrooms, leek, Worcestershire sauce, soy sauce, bay leaf and beef broth. Cover and cook on LOW 6 hours.

2. Stir in thawed mixed vegetables and barley. Cover and continue cooking on LOW 1 to 2 hours or until beef is fork-tender and barley is cooked. Remove bay leaf before serving.

Makes 8 servings

Slow Cooker Fish Stock

2 **tablespoons olive oil**

1 **large onion, chopped**

2 **carrots, chopped**

2 **stalks celery, chopped**

1 **cup white wine**

2 **whole tilapia, scaled and gutted**

8 **cups water**

1 **sprig thyme**

4 **sprigs parsley**

4 **whole black peppercorns**

2 **teaspoons salt**

1. Heat olive oil in skillet over medium-high heat. Add onion, carrots and celery. Cook until tender and lightly browned, 6 to 8 minutes. Add wine and scrape browned bits off bottom of pan. Pour mixture into **CROCK-POT®** slow cooker. Stir in remaining ingredients. Cover and cook on HIGH 3½ hours.

2. Skim off any foam; strain and let cool. Chill stock in refrigerator and remove fat that rises to surface.

Makes about 8 cups stock

Beef Barley Soup

Pork and Anaheim Stew

2 tablespoons extra-virgin olive oil, divided

1½ pounds boneless pork shoulder, fat trimmed, cut into ½-inch pieces

6 Anaheim peppers, halved lengthwise, seeded and sliced*

4 cloves garlic, minced

1 pound tomatillos, papery skins removed, rinsed and chopped

2 cups chopped onions

1 can (15½ ounces) yellow hominy, rinsed and drained

1 can (about 14 ounces) fat-free chicken broth

2 teaspoons chili powder

1 teaspoon ground cumin

1 teaspoon dried oregano

1½ teaspoons sugar

1 teaspoon liquid smoke

½ teaspoon salt plus more to taste

*Anaheim peppers can sting and irritate the skin, so wear rubber gloves when handling peppers and do not touch your eyes.

1. Heat 1 teaspoon olive oil in large skillet over high heat. Add half of pork and cook, stirring frequently, until browned on all sides. Transfer pork to **CROCK-POT®** slow cooker. Drain drippings from skillet and repeat with 1 teaspoon oil and remaining pork.

2. Reduce heat to medium-high. Add 1 teaspoon oil, turn ventilation fan to HIGH and add Anaheim peppers. Cook and stir 5 minutes or until peppers begin to brown on edges. Add garlic to peppers and cook 15 seconds, stirring constantly. Stir into pork in **CROCK-POT®** slow cooker. Stir in tomatillos, onions, hominy, chicken broth, chili powder, cumin, oregano and sugar. Cover and cook on LOW 10 hours or on HIGH 5 hours.

3. Stir in remaining 1 tablespoon oil, liquid smoke and salt. Serve immediately or cover and refrigerate overnight (flavors intensify with time).

Makes 4 servings

Northwest Beef and Vegetable Soup

2 **tablespoons olive oil**

1 **pound lean stew beef,
fat removed and cut into
1-inch cubes**

1 **medium onion, chopped**

1 **clove garlic, minced**

3½ **cups canned crushed
tomatoes, undrained**

1 **can (15 ounces) white
beans, drained and rinsed**

1 **buttercup squash, peeled
and diced**

1 **turnip, peeled and diced**

1 **large potato, peeled and
diced**

2 **stalks celery, sliced**

2 **tablespoons minced fresh
basil**

1½ **teaspoons salt**

1 **teaspoon black pepper**

8 **cups water**

1. Heat oil in skillet over medium heat until hot. Sear beef on all sides, turning as it browns. Add onion and garlic during last few minutes of searing. Transfer to **CROCK-POT®** slow cooker.

2. Add remaining ingredients. Gently stir well to combine. Cover; cook on HIGH 2 hours. Turn **CROCK-POT®** slow cooker to LOW. Cook on LOW 4 to 6 hours longer, stirring occasionally and adjusting seasonings to taste.

Makes 6 to 8 servings

Chuck and Stout Soup

2 tablespoons olive oil

3 pounds beef chuck, cut into 1-inch cubes

Kosher salt and black pepper

8 cups beef stock

3 large onions, thinly sliced

3 stalks celery, diced

6 carrots, peeled and diced

4 cloves garlic, peeled and minced

2 packages (10 ounces each) cremini mushrooms, thinly sliced

1 package (about 1 ounce) dried porcini mushrooms, processed to a fine powder

4 sprigs fresh thyme

1 bottle (12 ounces) stout beer

Flat-leaf parsley to garnish

Note: A coffee grinder works best for processing dried mushrooms, but a food processor or blender can also be used.

1. Heat oil in skillet over medium-high to high heat. Season meat with salt and pepper. In 2 batches, brown beef on all sides, taking care to not crowd meat. Meanwhile, in large saucepan, bring beef stock to a boil and reduce by half.

2. Remove beef and place in **CROCK-POT**® slow cooker. Add reduced stock and all remaining ingredients except parsley. Cover and cook on LOW 10 hours or on HIGH 6 hours.

3. Garnish with parsley and serve.

Makes 6 to 8 servings

Beef Stew

½ **cup all-purpose flour**

1 **teaspoon salt**

1 **teaspoon black pepper**

4 **pounds beef chuck,
cut into 1-inch cubes**

Olive oil

2 **cups red or white wine**

1 **cup beef broth**

2 **onions, sliced**

1 **cup sliced mushrooms**

1 **cup flat-leaf parsley,
minced**

6 **teaspoons minced garlic**

4 **whole bay leaves**

1. Mix flour, salt and pepper. Dredge beef in flour. Heat oil in skillet over medium heat until hot. Sear beef on all sides, turning as it browns. Transfer to **CROCK-POT®** slow cooker.

2. Add remaining ingredients and stir well to combine. Cover; cook on LOW 4 to 6 hours or on HIGH 2 to 3 hours.

Makes 6 to 8 servings

Mama's Beer Chili

- **2 tablespoons olive oil**
- **1 large onion (Vidalia if available), diced**
- **4 cloves garlic, crushed**
- **1½ to 2 pounds ground turkey**
- **1 can (28 ounces) crushed tomatoes**
- **1 cup beer (dark preferred)**
- **3 tablespoons chili powder**
- **1 teaspoon curry powder**
- **3 tablespoons hot pepper sauce**
- **⅓ cup honey**
- **1 package (10 ounces) frozen corn**
- **1 can (15 ounces) pink or kidney beans, rinsed and drained**
- **⅓ cup diced mild green chiles**
- **3 beef bouillon cubes**
- **1 to 2 tablespoons flour, to thicken**

Tip: Serve with cornbread and jam, or a loaf of fresh bread, if desired.

1. Heat oil in large skillet over medium-low heat until hot. Add onion. Cook and stir 5 minutes. Add garlic; cook and stir 2 minutes.

2. Add turkey to skillet. Cook and stir until turkey is no longer pink. Drain fat and discard.

3. Add remaining ingredients, stirring until mixed. Transfer to **CROCK-POT®** slow cooker. Cover; cook on LOW 8 to 10 hours or on HIGH 4 to 6 hours.

Makes 4 to 6 servings

Roast Pork Soup with Soba Noodles and Bok Choy

2 tablespoons hoisin sauce

1 tablespoon sugar

1 to 2 teaspoons Chinese five-spice powder

1 pork loin (about 2½ pounds)

6 cups chicken stock

1½ tablespoons fresh ginger, peeled and cut into thin slices

3 cloves garlic, thinly sliced

2 tablespoons soy sauce

1 head bok choy, sliced

1 pound soba noodles, cooked

1. Preheat oven to 350°F. In small bowl, combine hoisin sauce, sugar and five-spice powder. Baste pork with sauce and roast 45 to 60 minutes, or until just cooked through.

2. Let meat rest 15 minutes and slice into thin matchstick pieces.

3. Place pork in **CROCK-POT®** slow cooker and add stock, ginger, garlic, soy sauce and bok choy. Cover and cook on LOW 6 to 7 hours or on HIGH 3 to 4 hours.

4. Stir in soba noodles and cook until just heated through.

Makes 6 to 8 servings

Beef Bourguignon

6 **strips bacon, cut into
1- to 2-inch pieces**

3 **pounds beef rump roast,
cut into 1-inch cubes**

1 **large carrot, peeled and
sliced**

1 **medium onion, sliced**

1 **teaspoon salt**

½ **teaspoon black pepper**

3 **tablespoons all-purpose
flour**

1 **can (10 ounces)
condensed beef broth**

2 **cups red or Burgundy wine**

1 **pound fresh mushrooms,
sliced**

½ **pound small white onions,
peeled**

1 **tablespoon tomato paste**

2 **cloves garlic, minced**

½ **teaspoon dried thyme**

1 **whole bay leaf**

1. Cook bacon in skillet over medium heat until crisp. Remove; set aside.

2. Add beef to skillet and brown well. Remove; set aside.

3. Brown carrot and onion in skillet. Transfer to **CROCK-POT®** slow cooker. Season with salt and pepper. Stir in flour, add broth, and mix well. Stir in beef and bacon.

4. Add wine, mushrooms, onions tomato paste, garlic, thyme and bay leaf. Cover; cook on LOW 10 to 12 hours or HIGH 5 to 6 hours.

Makes 6 to 8 servings

Slow Cooker Vegetable Stock

3 **carrots, coarsely chopped**

3 **parsnips, coarsely chopped**

3 **onions, quartered**

3 **leeks, coarsely chopped**

3 **stalks celery, coarsely chopped**

3 **bay leaves**

2 **sprigs thyme**

4 **sprigs parsley**

8 **whole peppercorns**

Water

Kosher salt, to taste

Note: This recipe calls for bay leaves, thyme and parsley, but any combination of herbs and spices can be used to create a signature broth for a special soup such as Vietnamese Pho. Try a variety of classic herbs and spices such as rosemary, sage, parsley and chives, or experiment with more exotic varieties such as Thai basil, mint, cilantro, ginger, lemongrass and star anise. Varying the vegetables to suit the soup also offers limitless possibilities with additions such as turnip, sweet potato, yams, rutabaga, celery root, fennel or mushrooms.

1. Add all ingredients to **CROCK-POT**® slow cooker and fill three-quarters full with water. Season with salt. Cook on LOW 10 to 12 hours or on HIGH 6 to 8 hours.

2. Strain stock and discard solids. Allow stock to cool to room temperature and refrigerate, freeze or use immediately.

Makes 10 to 12 cups stock

Chicken and Black Bean Chili

1 **pound boneless, skinless chicken thighs, cut into 1-inch pieces**

2 **teaspoons chili powder**

2 **teaspoons ground cumin**

¾ **teaspoon salt**

1 **green bell pepper, diced**

1 **small onion, chopped**

3 **cloves garlic, minced**

1 **can (14½ ounces) diced tomatoes, undrained**

1 **cup chunky salsa**

1 **can (about 15 ounces) black beans, rinsed and drained**

Toppings: sour cream, diced ripe avocado, shredded Cheddar cheese, sliced green onions or chopped cilantro, crushed tortillas or corn chips

1. Combine chicken, chili powder, cumin and salt in **CROCK-POT®** slow cooker, tossing to coat.

2. Add bell pepper, onion and garlic; mix well. Stir in tomatoes with juice and salsa. Cover; cook on LOW 5 to 6 hours or on HIGH 2½ to 3 hours, or until chicken is tender.

3. Turn **CROCK-POT®** slow cooker to HIGH; stir in beans. Cover; cook 5 to 10 minutes or until beans are heated through. Ladle into shallow bowls; serve with desired toppings.

Makes 4 servings

Classic Chili

1½ **pounds ground beef**

1½ **cups chopped onion**

1 **cup chopped green bell pepper**

2 **cloves garlic, minced**

3 **cans (15 ounces each) dark red kidney beans, rinsed and drained**

2 **cans (15 ounces each) tomato sauce**

1 **can (14½ ounces) diced tomatoes, undrained**

2 **to 3 teaspoons chili powder**

1 **to 2 teaspoons dry hot mustard**

¾ **teaspoon dried basil**

½ **teaspoon black pepper**

1 **to 2 dried hot chili peppers (optional)**

1. Cook and stir ground beef, onion, bell pepper and garlic in large skillet until meat is browned and onion is tender. Drain fat and discard. Transfer mixture to **CROCK-POT®** slow cooker.

2. Add beans, tomato sauce, tomatoes with juice, chili powder, mustard, basil, black pepper and chili peppers, if desired; mix well. Cover; cook on LOW 8 to 10 hours or on HIGH 4 to 5 hours.

3. If used, remove chili peppers before serving.

Makes 6 servings

Chicken Fiesta Soup

- **4 boneless, skinless chicken breasts, cooked and shredded**
- **1 can (14½ ounces) stewed tomatoes, drained**
- **2 cans (4 ounces each) chopped green chilies**
- **1 can (28 ounces) enchilada sauce**
- **1 can (14½ ounces) chicken broth**
- **1 cup finely chopped onion**
- **2 cloves garlic, minced**
- **1 teaspoon ground cumin**
- **1 teaspoon chili powder**
- **¾ teaspoon black pepper**
- **1 teaspoon salt**
- **¼ cup finely chopped fresh cilantro**
- **1 cup frozen whole kernel corn**
- **1 yellow squash, diced**
- **1 zucchini, diced**
- **8 tostada shells, crumbled**
- **8 ounces shredded Cheddar cheese**

1. Combine chicken, tomatoes, chilies, enchilada sauce, broth, onion, garlic, cumin, chili powder, pepper, salt, cilantro, corn, squash and zucchini, in **CROCK-POT®** slow cooker.

2. Cover; cook on LOW 8 hours. To serve, fill individual bowls with soup. Garnish with crumbled tostada shells and cheese.

Makes 8 servings

Slow Cooker Beef or Veal Stock

3 to 4 tablespoons
vegetable oil, divided

3 to 4 pounds beef or veal
bones, preferably marrow
or knuckle bones

9 cups water, divided

2 large leeks, thoroughly
cleaned, cut into 1-inch
pieces

3 carrots, cut into 1-inch
pieces

3 cups onions, coarsely
chopped

2 stalks celery, cut into
1-inch pieces

1 tablespoon tomato paste

2 fresh thyme sprigs

2 large sprigs fresh flat-leaf
parsley

1 bay leaf

1/2 tablespoon black
peppercorns

**Note: To quickly cool down
stock for safe refrigerator
storage, pour strained stock
into a stockpot and place in
a sink or large bowl of ice,
stirring often.**

1. Preheat oven to 450°F. Coat large roasting pan with 1 to
2 tablespoons oil. Arrange bones in single layer in pan and roast
in middle of oven, turning once or twice, until browned, 30 to
45 minutes.

2. Using tongs, transfer bones to **CROCK-POT**® slow cooker.
Add 8 cups water. Discard fat from roasting pan, and add 1/2 cup
water to roasting pan, stirring and scraping up brown bits; add
to **CROCK-POT**® slow cooker. Cook on LOW 8 to 10 hours or on
HIGH 5 to 6 hours.

3. In last hour of slow cooking bones, preheat oven to 450°F.
Coat roasting pan with remaining 1 to 2 tablespoons oil and
arrange leeks, carrots, onions and celery in single layer. Roast
in middle of oven, stirring once or twice, until golden brown,
20 to 30 minutes. Transfer vegetables to **CROCK-POT**® slow
cooker and immediately add remaining 1/2 cup water to hot pan,
stirring and scraping up brown bits, then add to **CROCK-POT**®
slow cooker. Add tomato paste, thyme, parsley, bay leaf and
peppercorns; cook on HIGH 2 hours more.

4. Remove bones with tongs and discard. Pour stock in batches
through large sieve into stockpot and discard solids. Allow stock
to cool to room temperature and place in refrigerator overnight.
Before using or freezing, discard any fat that rises to top of
chilled stock.

Makes 8 to 10 cups stock

Vietnamese Chicken Pho

8 **cups chicken stock**

2 **to 3 cups cooked chicken, shredded**

8 **ounces bean sprouts**

Rice stick noodles

1 **bunch Thai basil, chopped**

Hoisin sauce, for serving

Lime wedges, for serving

Note: A simple soup to prepare with leftover shredded chicken, this classic Asian chicken noodle soup packs tons of flavor.

1. Add stock and chicken to **CROCK-POT®** slow cooker. Cover and cook on LOW 6 to 7 hours or on HIGH 3 hours.

2. Add bean sprouts, noodles and Thai basil. Heat until noodles are softened.

3. Spoon soup into individual serving bowls and serve with hoisin sauce and lime wedges.

Makes 4 to 6 servings

Beef and Lamb Entrées

Braised Fruited Lamb

- 6 tablespoons extra-virgin olive oil
- 4 pounds lamb shanks
- 2 tablespoons salt
- 2 tablespoons black pepper
- 1 cup dried apricots
- 1 cup dried figs
- 1½ cups water
- ½ cup white vinegar or white wine
- ¼ cup raspberry jam
- ½ teaspoon ground allspice
- ½ teaspoon ground cinnamon

1. Preheat broiler. Brush oil on lamb shanks and season with salt and pepper. Place shanks in broiler-safe pan and broil, turning to brown all sides, about 5 minutes per side. Remove from oven and transfer to **CROCK-POT**® slow cooker. Add dried apricots and figs.

2. Combine water, vinegar, jam, allspice and cinnamon in small bowl. Pour over lamb shanks. Cover; cook on LOW 8 to 9 hours or on HIGH 4 to 5 hours.

Makes 6 to 8 servings

Thai Steak Salad

Steak

- ¼ **cup soy sauce**
- 3 **cloves garlic, minced**
- 3 **tablespoons honey**
- 1 **pound boneless beef chuck steak, about ¾ inch thick**

Dressing

- ¼ **cup hoisin sauce**
- 2 **tablespoons creamy peanut butter**
- ½ **cup water**
- 1 **tablespoon minced fresh ginger**
- 1 **tablespoon ketchup or tomato paste**
- 2 **teaspoons lime juice**
- 1 **teaspoon sugar**
- 2 **cloves garlic, minced**
- ¼ **teaspoon hot chili sauce or sriracha***

Salad

- ½ **head savoy cabbage, shredded**
- 1 **bag (10 ounces) romaine lettuce with carrots and red cabbage**
- 1 **cup fresh cilantro leaves**
- ½ **cup chopped peanuts**
- ¾ **cup chopped mango**
  Fresh lime wedges

*Sriracha is a Thai hot sauce, sometimes called "rooster sauce" because of the label on the bottle, and is available in Asian specialty markets.

1. Prepare steak: Coat **CROCK-POT**® slow cooker with nonstick cooking spray. Combine soy sauce, garlic and honey in small bowl. Pour into **CROCK-POT**® slow cooker. Add steak, turning to coat. Cover; cook on HIGH 3 hours or until beef is tender.

2. Transfer beef to cutting board and let stand 10 minutes. Slice against the grain into ¼-inch strips. Cover with plastic wrap and refrigerate until needed.

3. Prepare dressing: Blend hoisin sauce and peanut butter until smooth. Add remaining dressing ingredients and mix until well blended.

4. Assemble salad: Toss cabbage and romaine salad mixture with dressing in large salad bowl. Top with reserved steak. Sprinkle with cilantro, peanuts and mango. Serve with lime wedges.

Makes 4 to 6 servings

**Beef and Lamb
Entrées**

Middle Eastern-Spiced Beef, Tomatoes and Beans

2 tablespoons extra-virgin olive oil, divided

1½ pounds lean boneless beef chuck roast, cut into 1-inch pieces, divided

1 can (14½ ounces) diced tomatoes with peppers and onions, undrained

6 ounces fresh green beans, trimmed and broken into 1-inch pieces

1 cup chopped onion

½ teaspoon ground cinnamon

¼ teaspoon ground allspice

1½ teaspoons sugar

¼ teaspoon garlic powder

½ teaspoon salt, or to taste

¼ teaspoon black pepper

Hot cooked rice or couscous (optional)

1. Heat 2 teaspoons oil in large skillet over medium-high heat. Add half of beef pieces and cook, stirring frequently, until browned on all sides. Transfer to **CROCK-POT®** slow cooker. Add additional 2 teaspoons oil and repeat with remaining beef.

2. Stir in tomatoes with juice, beans, onion, cinnamon, allspice, sugar and garlic powder. Cover and cook on LOW 8 hours or on HIGH 4 hours.

3. Stir in salt, pepper and remaining 2 teaspoons oil and let stand uncovered 15 minutes to allow flavors to absorb and thicken slightly. Serve as is or over cooked rice or couscous, if desired.

Makes about 4 servings

Polenta with Beef Chile Sauce

2 **tablespoons vegetable oil**

2 **pounds beef round roast,
cut into bite-size pieces**

1 **yellow onion, peeled and
finely chopped**

2 **cloves garlic, diced**

1³/₄ **cups water**

5 **canned whole green
chiles, peeled and diced***

1 **canned chipotle pepper in
adobo sauce, diced***

1 **teaspoon salt**

1 **teaspoon all-purpose
flour**

1 **teaspoon dried oregano**

¹/₂ **teaspoon ground cumin**

¹/₄ **teaspoon black pepper**

1 **package (16 ounces)
prepared polenta**

Fresh cilantro (optional)

*Green chiles and chipotle peppers
can sting and irritate the skin, so
wear rubber gloves when handling
peppers and do not touch your eyes.

1. Heat oil in large skillet over medium heat until hot. Sear beef on all sides, turning as it browns. Add onion and garlic during last few minutes of searing. Transfer to **CROCK-POT**® slow cooker.

2. Add water and chiles. Stir well to combine. Cover; cook on LOW 2 hours.

3. Combine salt, flour, oregano, cumin and black pepper in a small bowl. Add to **CROCK-POT**® slow cooker. Stir well to combine. Cover; cook on LOW 3 to 4 hours longer.

4. Turn **CROCK-POT**® slow cooker to WARM. Slice polenta in ¹/₂-inch-thick rounds. Place on greased baking sheet. Broil until crispy, about 4 minutes on each side.

5. To serve, place polenta rounds on individual plates and spoon meat and sauce over polenta. Garnish with fresh cilantro, if desired.

Makes 4 to 6 servings

Braised Chipotle Beef

3 **pounds chuck roast,
cut into 2-inch pieces**

1½ **teaspoons salt, plus
additional for seasoning
meat**

½ **teaspoon ground black
pepper, plus additional for
seasoning meat**

3 **tablespoons vegetable oil,
divided**

1 **large onion, cut into
1-inch pieces**

2 **red bell peppers, seeded
and cut into 1-inch pieces**

1 **tablespoon minced garlic**

1 **tablespoon chipotle chili
powder***

1 **tablespoon paprika**

1 **teaspoon dried oregano**

1 **tablespoon ground cumin**

3 **tablespoons tomato paste**

1 **cup beef broth**

1 **can (about 14 ounces)
diced tomatoes, drained**

Hot cooked rice (optional)

***Or substitute conventional chili
powder**

1. Pat beef dry with paper towels and season with salt and pepper. Heat 2 tablespoons oil in large skillet over medium-high heat. Working in batches, cook beef in skillet, turning to brown all sides. Transfer each batch to **CROCK-POT**® slow cooker as it is finished.

2. Return skillet to medium heat. Add remaining tablespoon oil. Add onion and cook, stirring occasionally, until just softened. Add bell peppers and cook 2 minutes. Stir in garlic, chili powder, paprika, oregano, cumin, tomato paste, 1½ teaspoons salt and ½ teaspoon pepper. Cook and stir 1 minute. Transfer to **CROCK-POT**® slow cooker.

3. Return skillet to heat and add beef broth. Cook, stirring to scrape up any browned bits. Pour over beef in **CROCK-POT**® slow cooker. Stir in tomatoes. Cover and cook on LOW 7 hours or until beef is tender. Skim fat from sauce. Serve over hot cooked rice, if desired.

Makes 4 to 6 servings

Osso Bucco

1 **large onion, cut into thin wedges**

2 **large carrots, sliced**

4 **cloves garlic, sliced**

4 **meaty veal shanks (3 to 4 pounds)**

2 **teaspoons herbes de Provence or ½ teaspoon each dried thyme, rosemary, oregano and basil**

1 **teaspoon salt**

½ **teaspoon black pepper**

¾ **cup canned beef consommé or beef broth**

¼ **cup dry vermouth (optional)**

3 **tablespoons all-purpose flour**

3 **tablespoons water**

¼ **cup minced parsley**

1 **small clove garlic, minced**

1 **teaspoon grated lemon peel**

1. Coat **CROCK-POT**® slow cooker with nonstick cooking spray. Place onion, carrots and sliced garlic in bottom. Arrange veal shanks over vegetables, overlapping slightly, and sprinkle herbes, salt and pepper over all. Add consommé and vermouth, if desired. Cover; cook on LOW 8 to 9 hours or on HIGH 5 to 6 hours or until shanks and vegetables are tender.

2. Transfer shanks and vegetables to serving platter; cover with foil to keep warm. Turn **CROCK-POT**® slow cooker to HIGH. Combine flour with water, mixing until smooth. Stir into cooking liquid. Cover; cook on HIGH 15 minutes or until sauce thickens.

3. Serve sauce over shanks and vegetables. Combine parsley, minced garlic and lemon peel; sprinkle over shanks and vegetables.

Makes 4 servings

Yankee Pot Roast and Vegetables

1 beef chuck pot roast (about 2½ pounds)

Salt and black pepper

3 unpeeled medium baking potatoes (about 1 pound), cut into quarters

2 large carrots, cut into ¾-inch slices

2 stalks celery, cut into ¾-inch slices

1 medium onion, sliced

1 large parsnip, cut into ¾-inch slices

2 bay leaves

1 teaspoon dried rosemary

½ teaspoon dried thyme

½ cup reduced-sodium beef broth

Tip: To make gravy, ladle cooking liquid into 2-cup measure; let stand 5 minutes. Skim off fat and discard. Measure remaining cooking liquid and heat to a boil in small saucepan. For each cup of cooking liquid, mix 2 tablespoons flour with ¼ cup cold water until smooth. Stir flour mixture into boiling cooking liquid, stirring constantly 1 minute or until thickened.

1. Trim excess fat from beef and discard. Cut beef into serving-size pieces; sprinkle with salt and pepper.

2. Combine potatoes, carrots, celery, onion, parsnip, bay leaves, rosemary and thyme in **CROCK-POT**® slow cooker. Place beef over vegetables. Pour broth over beef. Cover; cook on LOW 8½ to 9 hours, or until beef is fork-tender.

3. Transfer beef to serving platter. Arrange vegetables around beef. Remove and discard bay leaves before serving.

Makes 10 to 12 servings

Asian Short Ribs

½ **beef broth**

¼ **cup soy sauce**

¼ **cup dry sherry**

1 **tablespoon honey**

3 **teaspoons grated fresh ginger**

2 **teaspoons minced garlic**

3 **pounds boneless beef short ribs**

1 **teaspoon salt**

½ **teaspoon black pepper**

½ **cup chopped green onions (optional)**

Hot cooked rice

Tip: To mince ginger quickly, cut a small chunk, remove the skin and put through a garlic press. Store remaining unpeeled ginger in a plastic food storage bag in the refrigerator for up to 3 weeks.

1. Stir together beef broth, soy sauce, sherry, honey, ginger and garlic in **CROCK-POT®** slow cooker.

2. Season short ribs with salt and pepper. Place in **CROCK-POT®** slow cooker turning to coat all sides with sauce.

3. Cover and cook on LOW 7 to 8 hours or until meat is fork-tender.

4. Remove beef and place on serving dish. Garnish with green onions, if desired. Serve with cooked rice.

Makes 4 to 6 servings

Ginger Beef with Peppers and Mushrooms

1½ **pounds beef top round steak for London broil, cut into ¾-inch cubes**

24 **baby carrots**

1 **red bell pepper, seeded and chopped**

1 **green bell pepper, seeded and chopped**

1 **onion, chopped**

1 **package (8 ounces) fresh mushrooms, cut in halves**

2 **tablespoons grated fresh ginger**

1 **cup reduced-sodium beef broth**

½ **cup hoisin sauce**

¼ **cup quick-cooking tapioca**

Hot cooked white rice

Combine all ingredients except cooked rice in **CROCK-POT®** slow cooker. Cover and cook on LOW 8 to 9 hours. Serve over white rice.

Makes 6 servings

Tex-Mex Beef Wraps

1 **tablespoon chili powder**

2 **teaspoons ground cumin**

1 **teaspoon salt**

1/4 **teaspoon ground red pepper**

1 **boneless beef chuck pot roast (2½ to 3 pounds), cut into 4 pieces**

1 **medium onion, chopped**

3 **cloves garlic, minced**

1 **cup salsa, divided**

12 **(6- to 7-inch) flour or corn tortillas, warmed**

1 **cup shredded Cheddar or Monterey Jack cheese**

1 **cup chopped tomato**

1/4 **cup chopped cilantro**

1 **ripe avocado, diced**

1. Blend chili powder, cumin, salt and red pepper. Rub meat all over with spice mixture. Place onion and garlic in bottom of **CROCK-POT®** slow cooker; top with meat. Spoon 1/2 cup salsa over meat. Cover and cook on LOW 8 to 9 hours, or on HIGH 3½ to 4½ hours.

2. Remove meat from **CROCK-POT®** slow cooker; place on plate and use 2 forks to shred meat. Skim off and discard fat from cooking liquid; return meat to juices and mix well. Adjust seasonings. Place meat on warm tortillas; top with cheese, tomato, cilantro and avocado. Roll up to enclose filling. Serve with remaining salsa.

Makes 6 servings

Moroccan-Style Lamb Shoulder Chops with Couscous

**4 lamb blade chops
(about 2½ pounds)**

**Salt and black pepper,
to taste**

1 tablespoon olive oil

1 onion, chopped

1 clove garlic, minced

**1 teaspoon grated fresh
ginger**

**¼ teaspoon ground
cinnamon**

½ teaspoon ground turmeric

½ teaspoon salt

¼ teaspoon black pepper

1 bay leaf

**1 can (14½ ounces) diced
tomatoes, undrained**

**1 cup canned chickpeas,
rinsed and drained**

½ cup water

2 tablespoons lemon juice

Hot cooked couscous

Lemon wedges (optional)

**Tip: Adding fresh lemon
juice just before serving
enhances the flavor of many
dishes. Try it with other
dishes prepared in your
CROCK-POT® slow cooker.**

1. Coat **CROCK-POT®** slow cooker with nonstick cooking spray. Season lamb chops with salt and pepper. Heat oil in large skillet over medium-high heat until hot. Add lamb chops and brown on all sides. Transfer to **CROCK-POT®** slow cooker.

2. Add onion to skillet. Cook and stir 2 to 3 minutes or until translucent. Add garlic, ginger, cinnamon, turmeric, salt, pepper and bay leaf. Cook and stir 30 seconds longer. Stir in tomatoes with juice, chickpeas, water and lemon juice. Simmer 2 minutes. Pour mixture over lamb. Cover; cook on HIGH 3½ to 4 hours or until lamb is tender.

3. Add salt and pepper, if desired. Serve lamb chops over couscous with sauce and vegetables. Serve with lemon wedges, if desired.

Makes 4 servings

Shepherd's Pie

1 **pound lean ground beef**

1 **pound ground lamb**

1 **package (12 ounces) frozen chopped onions**

2 **teaspoons minced fresh garlic**

1 **can (about 14 ounces) diced tomatoes, drained**

1 **package (16 ounces) frozen peas and carrots**

3 **tablespoons quick-cooking tapioca**

2 **teaspoons dried oregano**

1 **teaspoon salt**

1/2 **teaspoon black pepper**

2 **packages (24 ounces each) prepared mashed potatoes**

1. Cook beef and lamb in large nonstick skillet over medium high heat, stirring occasionally, until no longer pink. Transfer to **CROCK-POT®** slow cooker. Return skillet to heat and add onion and garlic. Cook, stirring frequently, until onions begin to soften. Transfer to **CROCK-POT®** slow cooker with beef and lamb.

2. Stir in tomatoes, peas and carrots, tapioca, oregano, salt and pepper. Cover and cook on LOW 7 to 3 hours.

3. Top with prepared mashed potatoes. Cover and cook on LOW until potatoes are heated through, about 30 minutes.

Makes 6 servings

Beef with Apples and Sweet Potatoes

1 **boneless beef chuck shoulder roast (about 2 pounds)**

1 **can (40 ounces) sweet potatoes, drained**

2 **small onions, sliced**

2 **apples, cored and sliced**

1/2 **cup beef broth**

2 **cloves garlic, minced**

1 **teaspoon salt**

1 **teaspoon dried thyme, divided**

3/4 **teaspoon black pepper, divided**

1 **tablespoon cornstarch**

1/4 **teaspoon ground cinnamon**

2 **tablespoons cold water**

**Tip: Because CROCK-POT®
slow cookers cook at a low
heat for a long time, they're
a great way to cook dishes
calling for less-tender cuts
of meat since long, slow
cooking helps tenderize
these cuts.**

1. Trim excess fat from beef and discard. Cut beef into 2-inch pieces. Place beef, sweet potatoes, onions, apples, broth, garlic, salt, 1/2 teaspoon thyme and 1/2 teaspoon pepper in **CROCK-POT®** slow cooker. Cover; cook on LOW 8 to 9 hours.

2. Transfer beef, sweet potatoes and apples to platter; cover with foil to keep warm. Let cooking liquid stand 5 minutes to allow fat to rise. Skim off fat and discard.

3. Stir together cornstarch, remaining 1/2 teaspoon thyme, remaining 1/4 teaspoon pepper, cinnamon and water until smooth; stir into cooking liquid. Cook 15 minutes on HIGH or until cooking liquid is thickened. Serve sauce over beef, sweet potatoes and apples.

Makes 6 servings

Asian Beef with Broccoli

1½ **pounds boneless chuck steak, about 1½ inches thick, sliced into thin strips***

1 **can (10½ ounces) condensed beef consommé, undiluted**

½ **cup oyster sauce**

2 **tablespoons cornstarch**

1 **bag (16 ounces) fresh broccoli florets**

Hot cooked rice

Sesame seeds (optional)

*To make slicing steak easier, place in freezer for 30 minutes to firm.

1. Place beef in **CROCK-POT**® slow cooker. Pour consommé and oyster sauce over beef. Cover; cook on HIGH 3 hours.

2. Combine cornstarch and 2 tablespoons cooking liquid in small bowl. Add to **CROCK-POT**® slow cooker. Stir well to combine. Cover; cook on HIGH 15 minutes longer or until thickened.

3. Poke holes in broccoli bag with fork. Microwave on HIGH (100% power) 3 minutes. Empty bag into **CROCK-POT**® slow cooker. Gently toss beef and broccoli together. Serve over cooked rice. Garnish with sesame seeds, if desired.

Makes 4 to 6 servings

Italian-Style Pot Roast

2 **teaspoons minced garlic**

1 **teaspoon salt**

1 **teaspoon dried basil**

1 **teaspoon dried oregano**

¼ **teaspoon red pepper flakes**

1 **boneless beef bottom round rump or chuck shoulder roast (about 2½ to 3 pounds)**

1 **large onion, quartered and thinly sliced**

1½ **cups tomato-basil or marinara pasta sauce**

2 **cans (about 15 ounces each) cannellini or Great Northern beans, rinsed and drained**

¼ **cup shredded fresh basil**

1. Combine garlic, salt, basil, oregano and red pepper flakes in small bowl; rub over roast.

2. Place half of onion slices into **CROCK-POT®** slow cooker. (Cut roast in half to fit into smaller **CROCK-POT®** slow cooker.) Place one half of roast over onion slices; top with remaining onion slices and other half of roast (if using 4-quart slow cooker). Pour pasta sauce over roast. Cover; cook on LOW 8 to 9 hours or until roast is fork-tender.

3. Remove roast to cutting board; tent with foil. Let liquid in **CROCK-POT®** slow cooker stand 5 minutes to allow fat to rise. Skim off fat.

4. Stir beans into liquid. Cover; cook on HIGH 15 to 30 minutes or until beans are hot. Carve roast across the grain into thin slices. Serve with bean mixture and fresh basil.

Makes 6 to 8 servings

Classic Spaghetti

2 tablespoons olive oil

2 onions, chopped

2 green bell peppers, sliced

2 stalks celery, sliced

4 teaspoons minced garlic

3 pounds lean ground beef

2 carrots, diced

1 cup sliced mushrooms

1 can (28 ounces) tomato
sauce

1 can (28 ounces) stewed
tomatoes, undrained

3 cups water

2 tablespoons minced
parsley

1 tablespoon dried oregano

1 tablespoon sugar

2 teaspoons salt

2 teaspoons black pepper

1 pound uncooked spaghetti

1. Heat oil in large skillet over medium-high heat until hot. Add onions, bell peppers, celery and garlic; cook and stir until tender. Transfer to **CROCK-POT**® slow cooker.

2. In same skillet, brown ground beef. Drain and discard fat. Add beef, carrots, mushrooms, tomato sauce, tomatoes with juice, water, parsley, oregano, sugar, salt and black pepper to **CROCK-POT**® slow cooker. Cover; cook on LOW 6 to 8 hours or on HIGH 3 to 5 hours or until done.

3. Cook spaghetti according to package directions; drain. Serve sauce over cooked spaghetti.

Makes 6 to 8 servings

Beef and Lamb Entrées

Barbecue Roast Beef

2 **pounds boneless, cooked roast beef**

1 **bottle (12 ounces) barbecue sauce**

1½ **cups water**

10 **to 12 sandwich rolls, halved**

Tip: Freeze leftovers as individual portions; just reheat in a microwave for fast meals!

1. Combine roast beef, barbecue sauce and water in **CROCK-POT®** slow cooker. Cover; cook on LOW 2 hours.

2. Remove beef from **CROCK-POT®** slow cooker. Shred with 2 forks. Return beef to sauce; mix well. Serve on rolls.

Makes 10 to 12 sandwiches

Asian Beef with Mandarin Oranges

2 tablespoons vegetable oil

2 pounds boneless beef chuck, cut into ½-inch strips

1 small onion, thinly sliced

⅓ cup soy sauce

¼ teaspoon salt

2 teaspoons minced fresh ginger

1 small green bell pepper, sliced

1 package (about 3 ounces) shiitake mushrooms, sliced

1 head bok choy, cleaned and chopped

1 can (5 ounces) sliced water chestnuts, drained

2 tablespoons cornstarch

1 can (11 ounces) mandarin oranges, drained and syrup reserved

2 cups beef broth

6 cups steamed rice

1. Heat vegetable oil over medium-high heat. Add beef, in batches if necessary, and cook, turning to brown all sides. Transfer beef to **CROCK-POT®** slow cooker as it is browned.

2. Add onion to same skillet. Stir over medium heat until softened. Add soy sauce, salt, ginger, green pepper, mushrooms, bok choy and water chestnuts and cook until bok choy is wilted, about 5 minutes. Spoon mixture over beef.

3. Whisk together cornstarch and reserved mandarin orange syrup in medium bowl. Stir in beef broth and pour over ingredients in **CROCK-POT®** slow cooker. Cover and cook on LOW 10 hours or on HIGH 5 to 6 hours or until beef is tender.

4. Stir in mandarin oranges. Spoon steamed rice into shallow serving bowl and spoon beef over rice.

Makes 6 servings

Korean Barbecue Beef

4 to 4¹⁄₂ pounds beef short ribs

¹⁄₄ cup chopped green onions (white and green parts)

¹⁄₄ cup tamari or soy sauce

¹⁄₄ cup beef broth or water

1 tablespoon packed brown sugar

2 teaspoons minced fresh ginger

2 teaspoons minced garlic

¹⁄₂ teaspoon black pepper

2 teaspoons dark sesame oil

Hot cooked rice or linguine pasta

2 teaspoons sesame seeds, toasted

Tip: Three pounds of boneless short ribs can be substituted for the beef short ribs.

1. Place ribs in **CROCK-POT**® slow cooker. Combine green onions, tamari, broth, sugar, ginger, garlic and pepper in medium bowl; mix well and pour over ribs. Cover; cook on LOW 7 to 8 hours or until ribs are fork-tender.

2. Remove ribs from cooking liquid. Cool slightly. Trim excess fat and discard. Cut rib meat into bite-size pieces, discarding bones and fat.

3. Let cooking liquid stand 5 minutes to allow fat to rise. Skim off fat and discard.

4. Stir sesame oil into cooking liquid. Return beef to **CROCK-POT**® slow cooker. Cover; cook on LOW 15 to 30 minutes or until hot. Serve over rice; garnish with sesame seeds.

Makes 6 servings

Corned Beef and Cabbage

2 **onions, thickly sliced**

1 **corned beef brisket (about 3 pounds) with seasoning packet**

1 **package (8 to 10 ounces) baby carrots**

6 **medium potatoes, peeled and cut into wedges**

1 **cup water**

3 **to 5 slices bacon**

1 **head green cabbage, cut into wedges**

1. Layer onion slices to cover bottom of **CROCK-POT®** slow cooker. Add corned beef with seasoning packet, carrots and potato wedges. Pour 1 cup water over. Cover and cook on LOW 10 hours.

2. With 30 minutes left in cooking time, heat large saucepan over medium-high heat. Add bacon; cook and stir until bacon is crisp. Remove bacon with slotted spoon and drain on paper towels. When cool enough to handle, crumble bacon.

3. Place cabbage in saucepan with bacon drippings, cover with water. Bring to a boil and cook 20 to 30 minutes or until cabbage in tender. Drain.

4. Serve corned beef with vegetables. Top with crumbled bacon.

Makes 6 servings

Mediterranean Lamb Shanks

- **3 pounds lamb shanks**
- **Salt and black pepper, to taste**
- **All-purpose flour, as needed**
- **2 tablespoons olive oil**
- **1 medium red onion, chopped**
- **2 cloves garlic, minced**
- **2 cups red wine**
- **1 medium eggplant, peeled and cut into ½-inch cubes**
- **1 large red bell pepper, cored, seeded and sliced**
- **1 large tomato, seeded and chopped**
- **1 teaspoon dried thyme**
- **½ teaspoon dried rosemary**
- **2 cinnamon sticks**
- **½ cup kalamata olives, pitted**
- **2 tablespoons minced flat-leaf parsley**

1. Season lamb on both sides with salt and pepper, then lightly coat with flour. Heat oil in skillet over medium heat until hot. Sear lamb on all sides, 1 to 2 minutes per side, turning as it browns. Transfer to **CROCK-POT®** slow cooker.

2. Add onion and garlic to skillet. Cook and stir 3 to 4 minutes or until onion softens. Transfer to **CROCK-POT®** slow cooker.

3. Add wine, eggplant, bell pepper, tomato, thyme, rosemary and cinnamon to **CROCK-POT®** slow cooker. Stir well to combine. Cover; cook on LOW 7½ to 9½ hours or on HIGH 4½ to 6½ hours, or until meat is tender.

4. Remove cinnamon sticks before serving. Garnish with olives and parsley.

Makes 6 servings

Hungarian Lamb Goulash

1 package (16 ounces) frozen cut green beans, thawed

1 cup chopped onion

1¼ pounds lean lamb for stew, cut into 1-inch cubes

1 can (15 ounces) chunky tomato sauce

1¾ cups fat-free reduced-sodium chicken broth

1 can (6 ounces) tomato paste

4 teaspoons paprika

Hot cooked egg noodles

1. Place green beans and onion in **CROCK-POT®** slow cooker. Top with lamb.

2. Combine tomato sauce, broth, tomato paste and paprika in large bowl; mix well. Pour over lamb mixture. Cover; cook on LOW 6 to 8 hours. Stir goulash before serving over noodles.

Makes 6 servings

Chicken Entrées

Roast Chicken with Peas, Prosciutto and Cream

1 whole roasting chicken (about 2½ pounds), cut up

Salt and black pepper, to taste

5 ounces prosciutto, diced

1 small white onion, finely chopped

½ cup dry white wine

1 package (10 ounces) frozen peas

½ cup heavy cream

1½ tablespoons cornstarch

2 tablespoons water

4 cups farfalle pasta, cooked al dente

1. Season chicken pieces with salt and pepper. Combine chicken, prosciutto, onion and wine in **CROCK-POT®** slow cooker. Cover; cook on HIGH 3½ to 4 hours or on LOW 8 to 10 hours.

2. During last 30 minutes of cooking, add frozen peas and heavy cream to cooking liquid.

3. Remove chicken when done and no pink remains. Carve meat and set aside on a warmed platter.

4. Combine cornstarch and water. Add to cooking liquid in **CROCK-POT®** slow cooker. Cover; cook on HIGH 10 to 15 minutes or until thickened.

5. To serve, spoon pasta onto individual plates. Place chicken on pasta and top each portion with sauce.

Makes 6 servings

Chicken Marsala with Fettuccine

4 boneless, skinless chicken breasts

Salt and black pepper, to taste

1 tablespoon vegetable oil

1 onion, chopped

1/2 cup Marsala wine

2 packages (6 ounces each) sliced brown mushrooms

1/2 cup chicken broth

2 teaspoons Worcestershire sauce

1/2 teaspoon salt

1/2 teaspoon freshly ground black pepper

1/2 cup whipping cream

2 tablespoons cornstarch

8 ounces cooked fettuccine

2 tablespoons chopped fresh parsley

Tip: Skinless chicken is often the best choice for recipes using the CROCK-POT® slow cooker because the skin can shrivel and curl during cooking.

1. Coat **CROCK-POT®** slow cooker with nonstick cooking spray. Season chicken with salt and pepper. Transfer to **CROCK-POT®** slow cooker.

2. Heat oil in large skillet over medium heat until hot. Add onion. Cook and stir until translucent. Add Marsala and continue cooking 2 to 3 minutes until mixture reduces slightly. Stir in mushrooms. Add broth, Worcestershire sauce, 1/2 teaspoon salt and 1/2 teaspoon pepper. Pour mixture over chicken. Cover; cook on HIGH 1 1/2 to 1 3/4 hours or until chicken is done.

3. Transfer chicken to cutting board and let stand. Blend whipping cream and cornstarch until smooth. Stir into cooking liquid. Cover; cook 15 minutes longer or until mixture is thickened. Add salt and pepper, if desired.

4. Meanwhile, cook pasta according to directions on package. Drain and transfer to large serving bowl. Slice chicken breasts and place on pasta. Top with sauce and garnish with parsley.

Makes 6 to 8 servings

Hearty Cassoulet

1 **tablespoon olive oil**

1 **large onion, finely chopped**

4 **boneless, skinless chicken thighs (about 1 pound), chopped**

¼ **pound smoked turkey sausage, finely chopped**

3 **cloves garlic, minced**

1 **teaspoon dried thyme**

½ **teaspoon black pepper**

4 **tablespoons tomato paste**

2 **tablespoons water**

3 **cans (about 15 ounces each) Great Northern beans, rinsed and drained**

½ **cup dry bread crumbs**

3 **tablespoons minced fresh parsley**

Tip: When preparing ingredients for the CROCK-POT® slow cooker, cut into uniform pieces so that everything cooks evenly.

1. Heat oil in large skillet over medium heat until hot. Add onion; cook and stir 5 minutes or until onion is tender. Stir in chicken, sausage, garlic, thyme and pepper. Cook 5 minutes or until chicken and sausage are browned.

2. Remove skillet from heat; stir in tomato paste and water until blended. Place beans and chicken mixture in **CROCK-POT®** slow cooker. Cover; cook on LOW 4 to 4½ hours.

3. Before serving, combine bread crumbs and parsley in small bowl. Sprinkle over top of cassoulet.

Makes 6 servings

Chicken Saltimbocca-Style

- **6 boneless, skinless chicken breasts**
- **12 slices prosciutto**
- **12 slices provolone cheese**
- **½ cup all-purpose flour**
- **½ cup grated Parmesan cheese**
- **2 teaspoons salt**
- **2 teaspoons black pepper**
- **Olive oil**
- **2 cans (10¾ ounces each) condensed cream of mushroom soup, undiluted**
- **¾ cup white wine (optional)**
- **1 teaspoon ground sage**

1. Split each chicken breast into 2 thin pieces. Place between 2 pieces of waxed paper or plastic wrap. Pound until ⅓-inch thick. Place 1 slice of prosciutto and 1 slice of provolone on each chicken piece and roll up. Secure with toothpicks.

2. Combine flour, Parmesan cheese, salt and pepper, and place on plate. (This can be made up to 2 to 3 days in advance.) Coat chicken in flour mixture. Reserve excess flour mixture.

3. Heat oil in skillet over medium heat until hot. Brown chicken on both sides, turning as it browns. Transfer to **CROCK-POT**® slow cooker. Add soup, wine, if desired, and sage. Cover; cook on LOW 5 to 7 hours or on HIGH 2 to 3 hours.

4. To thicken sauce, stir in 2 to 3 tablespoons leftover flour mixture and cook 15 minutes longer before serving.

Makes 6 servings

Chicken and Baby Portobello Stroganoff

2½ **pounds boneless, skinless chicken thighs**

1 **pound baby portobello mushrooms, cleaned and sliced***

1 **cup frozen whole onions, thawed**

1 **can (10½ ounces) condensed French onion soup**

⅓ **cup dry sherry**

1 **tablespoon chopped fresh thyme or ½ teaspoon dried thyme**

½ **teaspoon black pepper**

½ **teaspoon coarse salt**

¼ **cup all-purpose flour**

2 **tablespoons butter, softened**

1 **cup sour cream**

Hot cooked egg noodles

Chopped fresh thyme (optional)

*Note: Baby portobellos (sometimes labelled "baby bellas") are available in the fresh produce section of many major supermarkets. Feel free to substitute an equal weight of any other fresh mushroom.

1. Place chicken, mushrooms and onions in **CROCK-POT**® slow cooker. Combine soup, sherry, thyme, pepper and salt in medium bowl. Pour over chicken and vegetables. Cover and cook on LOW 6 to 7 hours until chicken is fork-tender.

2. Combine flour and butter until smooth. Stir into cooking liquid in **CROCK-POT**® slow cooker and continue cooking 15 minutes or until thickened.

3. Stir in sour cream. Cover and cook 15 minutes more. Serve over egg noodles and sprinkle with thyme, if desired.

Makes 6 to 8 servings

Spanish Chicken with Rice

2	**tablespoons olive oil**
11	**ounces cooked linguiça or kielbasa, sliced into ½-inch rounds**
6	**boneless, skinless chicken thighs (about 1 pound)**
1	**onion, diced**
5	**cloves garlic, minced**
2	**cups converted long-grain white rice**
½	**cup diced carrots**
1	**red bell pepper, cored, seeded and diced**
½	**teaspoon salt**
¼	**teaspoon black pepper**
¼	**teaspoon saffron threads (optional)**
3½	**cups hot fat-free, reduced-sodium chicken broth**
½	**cup frozen peas, thawed**

1. Heat oil in medium skillet over medium heat until hot. Add sausage and brown on both sides. Transfer to **CROCK-POT**® slow cooker with slotted spoon.

2. Add chicken to skillet and brown on all sides. Transfer to **CROCK-POT**® slow cooker. Add onion to skillet, and cook and stir until soft. Stir in garlic and cook 30 seconds longer. Transfer to **CROCK-POT**® slow cooker.

3. Add rice, carrots, bell pepper, salt, black pepper and saffron, if desired. Pour broth over mixture. Cover; cook on HIGH 3½ to 4 hours.

4. Before serving, stir in peas. Cook 15 minutes or until heated through.

Makes 6 servings

East Indian Curried Chicken with Capers and Brown Rice

2 **cups ripe plum tomatoes, diced**

1 **cup artichoke hearts, drained and chopped**

1 **cup chicken broth**

1 **medium red onion, chopped**

⅓ **cup dry white wine**

¼ **cup capers, drained**

2 **tablespoons quick-cooking tapioca**

2 **teaspoons curry powder**

½ **teaspoon ground thyme**

¼ **teaspoon salt**

¼ **teaspoon black pepper**

1½ **pounds boneless, skinless chicken breasts**

4 **cups cooked brown rice**

1. Combine tomatoes, artichokes, broth, onion, wine and capers in **CROCK-POT®** slow cooker.

2. Combine tapioca, curry, thyme, salt and pepper in small bowl. Add to **CROCK-POT®** slow cooker. Stir well to combine. Add chicken. Spoon sauce over chicken to coat. Cover; cook on LOW 7 to 9 hours or on HIGH 3 to 4 hours.

3. Serve chicken and vegetables over rice. Spoon sauce over chicken.

Makes 6 servings

Cream Cheese Chicken with Broccoli

4 pounds boneless, skinless chicken breasts, cut into 1/2-inch pieces

1 tablespoon olive oil

1 package (1 ounce) Italian salad dressing mix

2 cups sliced mushrooms

1 cup chopped onion

1 can (10 3/4 ounces) condensed low-fat cream of chicken soup, undiluted

1 bag (10 ounces) frozen broccoli florets, thawed

1 package (8 ounces) low-fat cream cheese, cubed

1/4 cup dry sherry

Hot cooked pasta

Tip: Cream cheese can be messy or even difficult to cut into cubes. Try placing it in the freezer for 10 to 15 minutes to make it firmer and easier to cut.

1. Toss chicken with olive oil. Sprinkle with Italian salad dressing mix. Place in **CROCK-POT®** slow cooker. Cover; cook on LOW 3 hours.

2. Coat large skillet with nonstick cooking spray. Add mushrooms and onion; cook 5 minutes over medium heat or until onion is tender, stirring occasionally.

3. Add soup, broccoli, cream cheese and sherry to skillet; cook and stir until hot. Transfer to **CROCK-POT®** slow cooker. Cover; cook on LOW 1 hour. Serve chicken and sauce over pasta.

Makes 10 to 12 servings

Sweet and Sour Chicken

¼ **cup chicken broth**

2 **tablespoons low-sodium soy sauce**

2 **tablespoons hoisin sauce**

1 **tablespoon cider vinegar**

1 **tablespoon tomato paste**

2 **teaspoons packed brown sugar**

1 **clove garlic, minced**

¼ **teaspoon black pepper**

1 **pound boneless, skinless chicken thighs, cut into 1-inch pieces**

2 **teaspoons cornstarch**

2 **tablespoons minced chives**

Hot cooked rice

1. Combine broth, soy sauce, hoisin sauce, vinegar, tomato paste, brown sugar, garlic and pepper in **CROCK-POT**® slow cooker. Stir well to mix.

2. Add chicken thighs, and stir well to coat. Cover; cook on LOW 2½ to 3½ hours.

3. Remove chicken with slotted spoon, and keep warm. Combine cornstarch and 2 tablespoons cooking liquid in small bowl. Add to **CROCK-POT**® slow cooker. Stir in chives. Turn heat to HIGH. Stir 2 minutes or until sauce is slightly thickened. Serve chicken and sauce over rice.

Makes 4 servings

Greek Chicken Pitas
with Creamy Mustard Sauce

Filling

- 1 **medium green bell pepper, cored, seeded and sliced into ½-inch strips**
- 1 **medium onion, cut into 8 wedges**
- 1 **pound boneless, skinless chicken breasts, rinsed and patted dry**
- 1 **tablespoon extra-virgin olive oil**
- 2 **teaspoons dried Greek seasoning blend**
- ¼ **teaspoon salt**

Sauce

- ¼ **cup plain fat-free yogurt**
- ¼ **cup mayonnaise**
- 1 **tablespoon prepared mustard**
- ¼ **teaspoon salt**
- 4 **whole pita rounds**
- ½ **cup crumbled feta cheese**

Optional toppings: sliced cucumbers, sliced tomatoes, kalamata olives

1. Coat **CROCK-POT®** slow cooker with nonstick cooking spray. Place bell pepper and onion in bottom. Add chicken, and drizzle with oil. Sprinkle evenly with Greek seasoning and ¼ teaspoon salt. Cover; cook on HIGH 1¾ hours or until chicken is no longer pink in center (vegetables will be slightly tender-crisp).

2. Remove chicken and slice. Remove vegetables using slotted spoon.

3. Prepare sauce: Combine yogurt, mayonnaise, mustard and ¼ teaspoon salt in small bowl. Whisk until smooth.

4. Warm pitas according to package directions. Cut in half, and layer with chicken, sauce, vegetables and feta cheese. Top as desired.

Makes 4 servings

Chicken in Enchilada Sauce

1 **can (14½ ounces) diced
tomatoes with chipotle
chiles, undrained***

1 **can (10 ounces) enchilada
sauce**

1 **cup frozen or canned corn**

¼ **teaspoon ground cumin**

¼ **teaspoon black pepper,
or to taste**

1½ **pounds boneless, skinless
chicken thighs, cut into
bite-size pieces**

2 **tablespoons minced
cilantro**

½ **cup shredded pepper jack
cheese****

Sliced green onions

*If tomatoes with chipotle chiles
aren't available, use diced tomatoes
with chiles or plain diced tomatoes
plus ¼ teaspoon crushed red pepper
flakes.

**For a less spicy dish, use
Monterey Jack cheese.

1. Combine tomatoes with juice, enchilada sauce, corn, cumin, and pepper in **CROCK-POT**® slow cooker. Add chicken; mix well to combine. Cover; cook on LOW 6 to 7 hours.

2. Stir in cilantro. Spoon chicken and sauce into 4 bowls. Sprinkle each serving with 2 tablespoons cheese. Garnish with green onions, if desired.

Makes 4 servings

Chicken Parmesan with Eggplant

6 boneless, skinless chicken breasts

2 eggs

2 teaspoons salt

2 teaspoons black pepper

2 cups Italian bread crumbs

1/2 cup olive oil

1/2 cup (1 stick) butter

2 small eggplants, cut into 3/4-inch-thick slices

1 1/2 cups grated Parmesan cheese, divided

2 1/2 cups tomato-basil sauce, divided

1 pound sliced or shredded mozzarella cheese

1. Slice chicken breasts in half lengthwise. Cut each half lengthwise again to get 4 (3/4-inch) slices.

2. Combine eggs, salt and pepper in medium bowl. Place bread crumbs in separate bowl or on plate. Dip chicken in egg, then coat in bread crumbs.

3. Heat oil and butter in skillet over medium heat until hot. Brown breaded chicken on all sides, turning as pieces brown. Transfer to paper towel-lined plate to drain excess oil.

4. Layer eggplant on bottom of **CROCK-POT**® slow cooker. Add 3/4 cup Parmesan cheese and 1 1/4 cups sauce. Arrange chicken on sauce. Add remaining Parmesan cheese and sauce. Top with mozzarella cheese. Cover; cook on LOW 6 hours or on HIGH 2 to 4 hours.

Makes 6 to 8 servings

Cerveza Chicken Enchilada Casserole

2 cups water

1 stalk celery, chopped

1 small carrot, peeled and chopped

1 bottle (12 ounces) Mexican beer, divided

Juice of 1 lime

1 teaspoon salt

1½ pounds boneless, skinless chicken breasts

1 can (19 ounces) enchilada sauce, divided

7 ounces white corn tortilla chips

½ medium onion, chopped

3 cups shredded Cheddar cheese

Sour cream, sliced olives and cilantro (optional)

1. Heat water, celery, carrot, 1 cup beer, lime juice and salt in saucepan over high heat until boiling. Add chicken breasts; reduce heat to simmer. Cook until chicken is cooked through, about 12 to 14 minutes. Remove; cool and shred into bite-size pieces.

2. Spoon ½ cup enchilada sauce in bottom of **CROCK-POT®** slow cooker. Place tortilla chips in 1 layer over sauce. Cover with ⅓ shredded chicken. Sprinkle ⅓ chopped onion over chicken. Add 1 cup cheese, spreading evenly. Pour ½ cup enchilada sauce over cheese. Repeat layering process 2 more times, pouring remaining beer over casserole before adding last layer of cheese.

3. Cover and cook on LOW 3½ to 4 hours. Garnish with sour cream, sliced olives and cilantro, if desired.

Makes 4 to 6 servings

Chicken Teriyaki

1 **pound boneless, skinless chicken tenders**

1 **can (6 ounces) pineapple juice**

¼ **cup soy sauce**

1 **tablespoon sugar**

1 **tablespoon minced fresh ginger**

1 **tablespoon minced garlic**

1 **tablespoon vegetable oil**

1 **tablespoon molasses**

24 **cherry tomatoes (optional)**

2 **cups hot cooked rice**

Combine all ingredients except rice in **CROCK-POT**® slow cooker. Cover; cook on LOW 2 hours or until chicken is tender. Serve chicken and sauce over rice.

Makes 4 servings

Chicken with Italian Sausage

**10 ounces bulk mild or
hot Italian sausage**

**6 boneless, skinless chicken
thighs**

**1 can (about 15 ounces)
white beans, rinsed and
drained**

**1 can (about 15 ounces) red
beans, rinsed and drained**

1 cup chicken broth

1 medium onion, chopped

1 teaspoon black pepper

¹/₂ teaspoon salt

Chopped fresh parsley

1. Brown sausage in large skillet over medium-high heat, stirring to break up meat. Drain fat and discard. Spoon sausage into **CROCK-POT®** slow cooker.

2. Trim fat from chicken and discard. Place chicken, beans, broth, onion, pepper and salt in **CROCK-POT®** slow cooker. Cover; cook on LOW 5 to 6 hours.

3. Adjust seasonings, if desired. Slice each chicken thigh on the diagonal. Serve with sausage and beans. Garnish with parsley.

Makes 6 servings

Chicken and Wild Rice Casserole

2 slices bacon, chopped

3 tablespoons olive oil

1½ pounds chicken thighs, trimmed of excess skin

½ cup diced onion

½ cup diced celery

2 tablespoons Worcestershire sauce

¾ teaspoon salt

¼ teaspoon black pepper

½ teaspoon dried sage

1 cup converted long-grain white rice

1 package (4 ounces) wild rice

6 ounces brown mushrooms, wiped clean and quartered*

3 cups hot chicken broth, or enough to cover chicken

Salt and black pepper, to taste

2 tablespoons chopped parsley

*Use "baby bellas" or cremini mushrooms. Or, you may substitute white button mushrooms.

1. Microwave bacon on HIGH (100% power) 1 minute. Transfer to **CROCK-POT®** slow cooker. Add olive oil and spread evenly on bottom. Place chicken in **CROCK-POT®** slow cooker, skin side down. Add remaining ingredients in order given, except parsley. Cover; cook on LOW 3 to 4 hours, or until rice is tender.

2. Uncover and let stand 15 minutes. Add salt and pepper, if desired. Remove skin before serving, if desired. Garnish with chopped parsley.

Makes 4 to 6 servings

Chinese Cashew Chicken

1 **can (16 ounces) bean sprouts, drained**

2 **cups sliced cooked chicken**

1 **can (10¾ ounces) condensed cream of mushroom soup, undiluted**

1 **cup sliced celery**

½ **cup chopped green onions with tops**

1 **can (4 ounces) sliced mushrooms, drained**

3 **tablespoons butter**

1 **tablespoon soy sauce**

1 **cup whole cashews**

Hot cooked rice

Tip: For easier preparation, cut up the ingredients for this CROCK-POT® slow cooker recipe the night before. Don't place the CROCK-POT® stoneware in the refrigerator. Instead, wrap the chicken and vegetables separately, and store in the refrigerator.

1. Combine bean sprouts, chicken, soup, celery, onions, mushrooms, butter and soy sauce in **CROCK-POT®** slow cooker; mix well. Cover; cook on LOW 4 to 6 hours or on HIGH 2 to 3 hours.

2. Stir in cashews just before serving. Serve over rice.

Makes 4 servings

Provençal Lemon and Olive Chicken

2 **cups chopped onion**

8 **skinless chicken thighs (about 2½ pounds)**

1 **lemon, thinly sliced and seeds removed**

1 **cup pitted green olives**

1 **tablespoon olive brine from jar or white vinegar**

2 **teaspoons herbes de Provence**

1 **bay leaf**

½ **teaspoon salt**

⅛ **teaspoon black pepper**

1 **cup chicken broth**

½ **cup minced fresh parsley**

Note: To skin chicken easily, grasp skin with paper towel and pull away. Repeat with fresh paper towel for each piece of chicken, discarding skins and towels.

1. Place onion in **CROCK-POT®** slow cooker. Arrange chicken thighs over onion. Place lemon slice on each thigh. Add olives, brine, herbes de Provence, bay leaf, salt and pepper. Slowly pour in chicken broth.

2. Cover; cook on LOW 5 to 6 hours or on HIGH 3 to 3½ hours or until chicken is tender. Stir in parsley before serving.

Makes 8 servings

Chicken and Spicy Black Bean Tacos

1 can (15 ounces) black beans, rinsed and drained

1 can (10 ounces) tomatoes with mild green chiles, drained

1½ teaspoons chili powder

¾ teaspoon ground cumin

1 tablespoon plus 1 teaspoon extra-virgin olive oil, divided

12 ounces boneless, skinless chicken breasts, rinsed and patted dry

12 crisp corn taco shells

Optional toppings: shredded lettuce, diced tomatoes, shredded cheese, sour cream, ripe olives

1. Coat **CROCK-POT**® slow cooker with nonstick cooking spray. Add beans and tomatoes with chiles. Blend chili powder and cumin with 1 teaspoon oil and rub onto chicken breasts. Place chicken in **CROCK-POT**® slow cooker. Cover; cook on HIGH 1¾ hours.

2. Remove chicken and slice. Transfer bean mixture to bowl using slotted spoon. Stir in 1 tablespoon oil.

3. To serve, warm taco shells according to package directions. Fill with equal amounts of bean mixture and chicken. Top as desired.

Makes 4 servings

Forty-Clove Chicken

1 whole chicken (about
 3 pounds), cut up

 Salt and black pepper

1 to 2 tablespoons olive oil

¼ cup dry white wine

2 tablespoons chopped
 fresh parsley or
 2 teaspoons dried parsley
 flakes

2 tablespoons dry vermouth

2 teaspoons dried basil

1 teaspoon dried oregano

 Pinch red pepper flakes

40 cloves garlic (about
 2 heads), peeled*

4 stalks celery, sliced

 Juice and peel of 1 lemon

 Fresh herbs

*The whole garlic bulb is called a
head.

1. Remove skin from chicken. Sprinkle chicken with salt and pepper. Heat oil in large skillet over medium heat. Add chicken; brown on all sides. Remove to platter.

2. Combine wine, parsley, vermouth, basil, oregano and red pepper flakes in large bowl. Add garlic and celery; coat well. Transfer garlic and celery to **CROCK-POT**® slow cooker with slotted spoon. Add chicken to remaining herb mixture; coat well. Place chicken on top of celery mixture in **CROCK-POT**® slow cooker. Sprinkle lemon juice and peel over chicken. Cover; cook on LOW 6 hours.

3. Sprinkle with fresh herbs before serving.

Makes 4 to 6 servings

Chicken Sausage Pilaf

1 pound chicken or turkey sausage, casings removed

1 package (about 7 ounces) uncooked chicken-flavored rice and vermicelli pasta mix

4 cups chicken broth

2 stalks celery, diced

¼ cup slivered almonds

Salt and black pepper

1. Brown sausage in large skillet over medium-high heat, stirring to break up meat. Drain fat. Add rice and pasta mix to skillet. Cook and stir 1 minute.

2. Place mixture in **CROCK-POT®** slow cooker. Add broth, celery, almonds, salt and pepper to **CROCK-POT®** slow cooker; mix well.

3. Cover; cook on LOW 7 to 10 hours or on HIGH 3 to 4 hours or until rice is tender.

Makes 4 servings

Coq au Vin

2 cups frozen pearl onions, thawed

4 slices thick-cut bacon, crisp-cooked and crumbled

1 cup sliced button mushrooms

1 clove garlic, minced

1 teaspoon dried thyme

¹⁄₈ teaspoon black pepper

6 boneless, skinless chicken breasts (about 2 pounds)

¹⁄₂ cup dry red wine

³⁄₄ cup reduced-sodium chicken broth

¹⁄₄ cup tomato paste

3 tablespoons all-purpose flour

Hot cooked egg noodles (optional)

Tip: Coq au Vin is a classic French dish that is made with bone-in chicken, salt pork or bacon, brandy, red wine and herbs. The dish originated when farmers needed a way to cook old chickens that could no longer breed. A slow, moist cooking method was needed to tenderize the tough old birds.

1. Layer onions, bacon, mushrooms, garlic, thyme, pepper, chicken, wine and broth in **CROCK-POT**® slow cooker.

2. Cover; cook on LOW 6 to 8 hours.

3. Remove chicken and vegetables; cover and keep warm. Ladle ¹⁄₂ cup cooking liquid into small bowl; cool slightly. Mix reserved liquid, tomato paste and flour until smooth; stir into **CROCK-POT**® slow cooker. Cook, uncovered, on HIGH 15 minutes or until thickened. Serve over hot noodles, if desired.

Makes 6 servings

Fish and Seafood Entrées

Braised Sea Bass with Aromatic Vegetables

2 tablespoons butter
or olive oil

2 bulbs fennel, thinly sliced

3 large carrots, julienned

3 large leeks, cleaned and
thinly sliced

Kosher salt and black
pepper

6 fillets sea bass or other
firm-fleshed white fish
(2 to 3 pounds total)

1. Melt butter in large skillet over medium-high heat. Add fennel, carrots and leeks. Cook and stir until beginning to soften and lightly brown. Season with salt and pepper.

2. Arrange half of vegetables in bottom of **CROCK-POT**® slow cooker.

3. Season fish with salt and pepper and place on vegetables in **CROCK-POT**® slow cooker. Top with remaining vegetables.

4. Cover and cook on LOW 2 to 3 hours or on HIGH 1 to 1½ hours or until fish is cooked through.

Makes 6 servings

Fish and Seafood Entrées

Seafood Bouillabaisse

½ **bulb fennel, chopped**

1 **medium onion, chopped**

2 **cloves garlic, minced**

2 **bottles (12 ounces each) beer, divided**

1 **can (28 ounces) tomato purée**

8 **ounces clam juice**

1 **bay leaf**

½ **teaspoon salt**

¼ **teaspoon black pepper**

2 **cups water**

½ **pound red snapper, pin bones removed and cut into 1-inch pieces**

8 **mussels, scrubbed and debearded**

8 **cherry stone clams**

8 **large shrimp, unpeeled**

4 **lemon wedges**

Italian parsley sprigs (optional)

1. To prepare tomato broth, cook fennel, onion and garlic in large skillet over medium-high heat until onion is soft and translucent. Transfer mixture to **CROCK-POT®** slow cooker, pour 1 bottle of beer, tomato purée, clam juice, bay leaf, salt and pepper in **CROCK-POT®** slow cooker. Cover, cook on LOW 6 to 8 hours or on HIGH 3 to 4 hours.

2. During last 30 minutes of cooking, pour remaining 1 bottle of beer into large stockpot. Add water. Place steamer insert in stockpot (do not allow water to touch the insert). Bring to boil. Place fish and shellfish into insert. Cover and steam for 4 to 8 minutes, discarding any mussels or clams that do not open.

3. Remove bay leaf from tomato broth. Ladle broth into wide soup bowls. Place mussels, clams, shrimp and fish on top. Squeeze lemon over fish and seafood. Garnish with parsley, if desired.

Makes 4 servings

Shrimp Jambalaya

- **1 can (28 ounces) diced tomatoes, undrained**
- **1 medium onion, chopped**
- **1 medium red bell pepper, chopped**
- **1 stalk celery, chopped**
- **2 tablespoons minced garlic**
- **2 teaspoons dried parsley flakes**
- **2 teaspoons dried oregano**
- **1 teaspoon hot pepper sauce**
- **1/2 teaspoon dried thyme**
- **2 pounds cooked large shrimp**
- **2 cups uncooked instant rice**
- **2 cups fat-free reduced-sodium chicken broth**

Tip: Seafood is delicate and should be added to the CROCK-POT® slow cooker during the last 15 to 30 minutes of the cooking time on HIGH, and during the last 30 to 45 minutes on the LOW setting. Seafood overcooks easily, becoming tough and rubbery, so watch your cooking times, and cook only long enough for seafood to be done.

1. Combine tomatoes with juice, onion, bell pepper, celery, garlic, parsley, oregano, hot sauce and thyme in **CROCK-POT®** slow cooker. Cover; cook on LOW 8 hours or on HIGH 4 hours.

2. Stir in shrimp. Cover; cook on LOW 20 minutes.

3. Meanwhile, prepare rice according to package directions, substituting broth for water. Serve jambalaya over hot cooked rice.

Makes 6 servings

**Fish and
Seafood
Entrées**

Cod Tapenade

**4 cod fillets, or other
firm-fleshed white fish
(2 to 3 pounds total)**

Salt and black pepper

2 lemons, thinly sliced

Tapenade (recipe follows)

1. Season fish with salt and pepper.

2. Arrange half lemon slices in bottom of **CROCK-POT**® slow cooker. Top with fish. Cover fish with remaining lemon slices. Cover. Cook on HIGH 1 hour or until fish is just cooked through (actual time depends on thickness of fish).

3. Remove fish to serving plates; discard lemon. Top with Tapenade.

Makes 4 servings

Tapenade

**½ pound pitted kalamata
olives**

**2 tablespoons anchovy
paste**

**2 tablespoons capers,
drained**

1 clove garlic

**⅛ teaspoon ground
red pepper**

**¼ teaspoon grated
orange zest**

**2 tablespoons chopped
fresh thyme or flat-leaf
parsley**

½ cup olive oil

Place all ingredients except oil in food processor. Pulse to roughly chop. Add oil and pulse briefly to form a chunky paste.

Fish and Seafood Entrées

Scallops in Fresh Tomato and Herb Sauce

2 tablespoons vegetable oil

1 medium red onion, peeled and diced

1 clove garlic, minced

3½ cups fresh tomatoes, peeled*

1 can (12 ounces) tomato purée

1 can (6 ounces) tomato paste

¼ cup dry red wine

2 tablespoons chopped flat-leaf parsley

1 tablespoon chopped fresh oregano

¼ teaspoon black pepper

1½ pounds fresh scallops, cleaned and drained

*To peel tomatoes, place one at a time in simmering water about 10 seconds. (Add 30 seconds if tomatoes are not fully ripened.) Immediately plunge into a bowl of cold water for another 10 seconds. Peel skin with a knife.

1. Heat oil in skillet over medium heat until hot. Add onion and garlic. Cook and stir 7 to 8 minutes, or until onions are soft and translucent. Transfer to **CROCK-POT®** slow cooker.

2. Add tomatoes, tomato purée, tomato paste, wine, parsley, oregano and pepper. Cover; cook on LOW 6 to 8 hours.

3. Turn **CROCK-POT®** slow cooker to HIGH. Add scallops. Cook on HIGH 15 minutes longer or until scallops are just cooked through. Serve over pasta or rice.

Makes 4 servings

Saffron-Scented Shrimp Paella

3 tablespoons olive oil, divided

1½ cups chopped onions

4 cloves garlic, sliced thin

Salt, to taste

1 cup roasted red bell pepper, diced

1 cup chopped tomato

1 whole bay leaf

1 large pinch saffron

1 cup white wine

8 cups chicken broth

4 cups rice

25 large shrimp, peeled, deveined and cleaned

Salt and white pepper, to taste

1. Heat 2 tablespoons oil in large skillet over medium heat until hot. Add onions, garlic and salt, to taste. Cook and stir until translucent, about 5 minutes. Add bell pepper, tomato, bay leaf and saffron. Cook and stir until heated through. Add wine. Continue cooking until liquid has reduced by half. Add broth. Bring to a simmer. Adjust seasonings, if desired and stir in rice. Transfer to **CROCK-POT**® slow cooker. Cover; cook on HIGH 30 minutes to 1 hour, or until rice has absorbed all of liquid.

2. Toss shrimp in remaining 1 tablespoon olive oil, and season with salt and white pepper. Place shrimp on rice in **CROCK-POT**® slow cooker. Cover; cook about 10 minutes, or until shrimp are just cooked through.

Makes 4 to 6 servings

Sweet and Sour Shrimp with Pineapple

3 **cans (8 ounces each) pineapple chunks, drained and 1 cup juice reserved**

2 **packages (6 ounces each) frozen snow peas, thawed**

¼ **cup cornstarch**

⅓ **cup sugar, plus 2 teaspoons**

2 **chicken bouillon cubes**

2 **cups boiling water**

4 **teaspoons soy sauce**

1 **teaspoon ground ginger**

1 **pound shrimp, peeled, deveined and cleaned***

¼ **cup cider vinegar**

Hot cooked rice

*Note: Or 1 pound frozen, peeled, deveined shrimp, unthawed

1. Drain pineapple chunks, reserving 1 cup juice. Place pineapple and snow peas in **CROCK-POT®** slow cooker.

2. Combine cornstarch and sugar in medium saucepan. Dissolve bouillon cubes in water and add to saucepan. Mix in 1 cup reserved pineapple juice, soy sauce and ginger. Bring to a boil and cook for 1 minute. Pour into **CROCK-POT®** slow cooker. Cover; cook on LOW 4½ to 5½ hours.

3. Add shrimp and vinegar. Cover; cook on LOW 30 minutes or until shrimp are done. Serve over hot rice.

Makes 4 servings

Cheesy Shrimp on Grits

1 cup finely chopped green bell pepper

1 cup finely chopped red bell pepper

1/2 cup thinly sliced celery

1 bunch green onions, chopped, divided

1/4 cup (1/2 stick) butter, cubed

1 1/4 teaspoons seafood seasoning

2 bay leaves

1/4 teaspoon ground red pepper

1 pound uncooked shrimp, peeled, deveined and cleaned

5 1/3 cups water

1 1/3 cups quick-cooking grits

8 ounces shredded sharp Cheddar cheese

1/4 cup whipping cream or half-and-half

Variation: This dish is also delicious served over polenta.

1. Coat **CROCK-POT**® slow cooker with nonstick cooking spray. Add bell peppers, celery, all but 1/2 cup green onions, butter, seafood seasoning, bay leaves and ground red pepper. Cover; cook on LOW 4 hours or on HIGH 2 hours.

2. Turn **CROCK-POT**® slow cooker to HIGH. Add shrimp. Cover; cook 15 minutes longer. Meanwhile, bring water to a boil in medium saucepan. Add grits and cook according to directions on package.

3. Discard bay leaves from shrimp mixture. Stir in cheese, cream and remaining 1/2 cup green onions. Cook 5 minutes longer or until cheese has melted. Serve over grits.

Makes 6 servings

Shrimp Creole

¼ cup (½ stick) butter

1 onion, chopped

¼ cup biscuit baking mix

3 cups water

1 cup chopped celery

1 cup chopped green bell pepper

2 cans (6 ounces each) tomato paste

2 teaspoons salt

½ teaspoon sugar

2 bay leaves

Black pepper, to taste

4 pounds shrimp, peeled, deveined and cleaned

Hot cooked rice

1. Cook and stir butter and onion in medium skillet over reduced heat until onion is tender. Stir in biscuit mix. Place mixture in **CROCK-POT**® slow cooker.

2. Add water, celery, bell pepper, tomato paste, salt, sugar, bay leaves and black pepper. Cover; cook on LOW 6 to 8 hours.

3. Turn **CROCK-POT**® slow cooker to HIGH and add shrimp. Cook on HIGH 45 minutes to 1 hour or until shrimp are done. Remove bay leaves. Serve over rice.

Makes 8 to 10 servings

Salmon with Beer

4 salmon fillets (6 ounces each)

Salt and black pepper

1 cup Italian dressing

3 tablespoons olive oil

1 yellow bell pepper, sliced

1 red bell pepper, sliced

1 orange bell pepper, sliced

1 large onion, sliced

1/2 teaspoon dried basil

2 cloves garlic, minced

1 teaspoon lemon peel

2 cups spinach, stems removed

3/4 cup amber ale

1/2 lemon, cut into quarters

Additional salt and black pepper (optional)

1. Season both sides of fillets with salt and black pepper. Place in casserole and pour Italian dressing over fillets. Cover and refrigerate 30 minutes, or up to 2 hours. Discard marinade.

2. Pour oil into **CROCK-POT**® slow cooker and lay salmon fillets on top, stacking as necessary. Top with peppers, onion, basil, garlic and lemon peel. Cover with spinach. Pour beer over top. Cover; cook on HIGH 1 1/2 hours.

3. Remove fillets to platter and top with vegetables. Squeeze lemon over salmon and season with additional salt and pepper, if desired.

Makes 4 servings

Hoppin' John

1 **package (1 pound) andouille or smoked sausage, sliced**

2½ **cups chicken broth, divided**

2 **cans (15 ounces each) black-eyed peas, rinsed and drained**

1 **box (about 8 ounces) dirty rice mix**

½ **cup salsa**

½ **to ¾ cup lump crabmeat (optional)**

1. Cook sausage in large skillet over medium heat, stirring frequently, 5 minutes or until browned all over. Transfer to **CROCK-POT®** slow cooker with slotted spoon; discard any drippings from pan. Return skillet to heat and pour in ½ cup chicken broth. Cook and stir scraping up any browned bits from skillet. Pour over sausage.

2. Stir black-eyed peas, rice mix, remaining chicken broth and salsa into **CROCK-POT®** slow cooker with sausage. Cover and cook on LOW 3 to 4 hours or until rice is tender. Add crabmeat, if desired, and stir until well combined. Cover and cook until heated through, about 5 minutes.

Makes 6 servings

Caribbean Shrimp with Rice

1 package (12 ounces)
frozen shrimp, thawed

½ cup fat-free, reduced-
sodium chicken broth

1 clove garlic, minced

1 teaspoon chili powder

½ teaspoon salt

½ teaspoon dried oregano

1 cup frozen peas, thawed

½ cup diced tomatoes

2 cups cooked long-grain
white rice

1. Combine shrimp, broth, garlic, chili powder, salt and oregano in **CROCK-POT®** slow cooker. Cover; cook on LOW 2 hours.

2. Add peas and tomatoes. Cover; cook on LOW 5 minutes. Stir in rice. Cover; cook on LOW 5 minutes longer, or until rice is heated through.

Makes 4 servings

Seafood and Tomato Herb Ragout

- **1 can (28 ounces) crushed tomatoes, undrained**
- **1 can (8 ounces) tomato sauce**
- **1 cup water**
- **1 cup white wine**
- **1 leek, chopped**
- **1 small green bell pepper, cored, seeded and chopped**
- **½ cup chopped celery**
- **⅓ cup chopped flat-leaf parsley**
- **¼ cup extra-virgin olive oil**
- **3 cloves garlic, minced**
- **2 tablespoons chopped fresh basil**
- **1 tablespoon chopped fresh thyme**
- **1 tablespoon chopped fresh oregano**
- **1 teaspoon salt**
- **½ teaspoon paprika**
- **¼ teaspoon crushed red pepper**
- **1 pound orange roughy fillets or other white fish such as cod or haddock, cubed**
- **12 prawns, peeled, deveined and cleaned**
- **12 scallops, cleaned**
- **Fresh parsley (optional)**

1. Place all ingredients except fish, prawns and scallops in **CROCK-POT**® clow cooker. Stir well to combine. Cover; cook on LOW 6 to 8 hours or on HIGH 3 to 4 hours.

2. Turn **CROCK-POT**® slow cooker to HIGH. Add fish, prawns and scallops. Cook 15 to 30 minutes longer, or until seafood is just cooked through. Garnish with parsley, if desired.

Makes 6 to 8 servings

Mom's Tuna Casserole

2 **cans (12 ounces each) tuna, drained and flaked**

3 **cups diced celery**

3 **cups crushed potato chips, divided**

6 **hard-cooked eggs, chopped**

1 **can (10¾ ounces) condensed cream of mushroom soup, undiluted**

1 **can (10¾ ounces) condensed cream of celery soup, undiluted**

1 **cup mayonnaise**

1 **teaspoon dried tarragon**

1 **teaspoon black pepper**

1. Combine tuna, celery, 2½ cups potato chips, eggs, soups, mayonnaise, tarragon and pepper in **CROCK-POT**® slow cooker; stir well. Cover; cook on LOW 5 to 8 hours.

2. Sprinkle with remaining ½ cup potato chips before serving.

Makes 8 servings

Pork Entrées

Pulled Pork with Cola Barbecue Sauce

1 teaspoon vegetable oil

3 pounds boneless pork shoulder roast, cut into 4 equal large pieces

1 cup cola

¼ cup tomato paste

2 tablespoons packed brown sugar

2 teaspoons Worcestershire sauce

2 teaspoons spicy brown mustard

Hot pepper sauce

Salt

8 hamburger buns

1. Heat oil in large skillet over medium-high heat. Add pork and cook, turning occasionally, until browned on all sides. Transfer pork to **CROCK-POT**® slow cooker as it is finished. Pour cola over pork. Cover; cook on LOW 7½ to 8 hours or on HIGH 3½ to 4 hours, until pork is fork-tender.

2. Remove pork to plate. Tent with foil and set aside.

3. Skim fat from cooking juices (or transfer to fat separator, pour off cooking juices, and discard fat). Pour into medium saucepan. Whisk in tomato paste, brown sugar, Worcestershire sauce and mustard. Bring to boil over high heat. Boil, whisking occasionally, until thickened and reduced to about 1 cup.

4. Shred pork with 2 forks. Stir pork into saucepan. Season to taste with hot pepper sauce and salt. Serve shredded pork on buns.

Makes 8 servings

Rigatoni with Broccoli Rabe and Sausage

2 tablespoons olive oil, plus more for oiling stoneware insert

3 sweet or hot Italian sausage links, casings removed

2 cloves garlic, minced

1 large bunch (about 1¼ pounds) broccoli rabe

½ cup chicken broth or water

½ teaspoon salt

½ teaspoon red pepper flakes

1 pound rigatoni

Grated Parmesan cheese (optional)

1. Lightly coat interior of **CROCK-POT**® slow cooker with nonstick cooking spray. Set aside.

2. Heat oil in large skillet over medium heat. Add sausage and cook, stirring to break up sausage with spoon, until lightly browned, about 6 minutes. Add garlic and stir until softened and fragrant, about 1 minute. Transfer to lightly prepared **CROCK-POT**® slow cooker.

3. Trim any stiff, woody parts from bottoms of broccoli rabe stems and discard. Cut broccoli rabe into 1-inch lengths. Place in large bowl of cold water. Stir with hands to wash well. Lift broccoli rabe out of water by handfuls leaving any sand or dirt in bottom of bowl. Shake well to remove excess water, but do not dry. Add to **CROCK-POT**® slow cooker with sausage. Pour in broth and sprinkle with salt and red pepper flakes. Cover; cook on LOW 4 hours or on HIGH 2 hours.

4. Meanwhile, cook rigatoni according to package directions. Stir into sausage mixture just before serving. Serve garnished, as desired, with Parmesan cheese.

Makes 6 servings

Green Chile Pulled Pork Sandwiches

3½ to 4 pounds pork shoulder

1 teaspoon salt

½ teaspoon ground black pepper

1 can (14½ ounces) diced tomatoes with green chiles, undrained

1 cup chopped onion

½ cup water

2 tablespoons fresh lime juice

1 teaspoon ground cumin

1 teaspoon minced garlic

2 chipotle peppers in adobo sauce, minced

8 hard rolls or hoagie buns

½ cup sour cream (optional)

2 ripe avocados, peeled, pitted and sliced (optional)

3 tablespoons chopped fresh cilantro (optional)

1. Season pork with salt and pepper and place in **CROCK-POT®** slow cooker.

2. Combine tomatoes and their juices, onion, water, lime juice, cumin, garlic and chipotle peppers in medium bowl. Pour over pork. Cover and cook on LOW 7 to 8 hours or until pork shreds easily when poked with fork or spoon.

3. Remove pork from cooking liquid and cool slightly. Remove any fat from surface of meat and discard. Pull pork apart into shreds with forks. Return pork to cooking liquid and stir to combine. Serve on rolls, topping each sandwich with about 1 tablespoon sour cream, a few avocado slices and a pinch of chopped cilantro or as desired.

Makes 8 servings

Ham and Cheese Pasta Bake

6 **cups water**

2 **teaspoons salt**

12 **ounces uncooked rigatoni**

1 **ham steak, cubed**

1 **container (10 ounces) refrigerated light Alfredo sauce**

2 **cups mozzarella cheese, divided**

2 **cups hot half-and-half**

1 **tablespoon cornstarch**

1. Bring water to a boil in medium saucepan. Stir in salt. Add rigatoni and boil 7 minutes. Drain well and transfer to **CROCK-POT®** slow cooker.

2. Stir in ham, Alfredo sauce and 1 cup mozzarella cheese. Whisk together half-and-half and cornstarch in small bowl. Pour half-and-half mixture over pasta to cover. Sprinkle on remaining cheese. Cover; cook on LOW 3½ to 4 hours. (Dish is done when rigatoni is tender and excess liquid is absorbed.)

Makes 6 servings

Savory Sausage Bread Pudding

4 **eggs**

2 **cups milk or 1 cup half-and-half and 1 cup milk**

¼ **teaspoon salt**

¼ **teaspoon black pepper**

¼ **teaspoon crushed dried thyme**

⅛ **teaspoon crushed red pepper flakes**

1 **package (10 ounces) smoky breakfast sausage links, cut into ½-inch pieces**

¾ **cup shredded Cheddar cheese**

2 **cups day-old bread cubes, cut into ½-inch pieces**

1. Beat eggs in large bowl. Add milk, salt, pepper, thyme and red pepper flakes; stir well. Stir in sausage, cheese and bread. Press bread into egg mixture. Set aside 10 minutes or until bread has absorbed liquid.

2. Generously butter 2-quart baking dish that fits inside **CROCK-POT®** slow cooker. Pour sausage mixture into baking dish. Cover dish with buttered foil, butter side down.

3. Pour 1 inch hot water into **CROCK-POT®** slow cooker. Add baking dish. Cover; cook on LOW 4 to 5 hours or until tester inserted into center comes out clean.

Makes 4 to 6 servings

Ham and Cheese Pasta Bake

Pork Chops with Jalapeño-Pecan Cornbread Stuffing

 6 **1-inch thick boneless pork loin chops (about 1½ pounds total)**

 ¾ **cup chopped onion**

 ¾ **cup chopped celery**

 ½ **cup coarsely chopped pecans**

 ½ **medium jalapeño pepper, seeded and chopped***

 1 **teaspoon rubbed sage**

 ½ **teaspoon dried rosemary**

 ⅛ **teaspoon black pepper**

 4 **cups unseasoned cornbread stuffing mix**

 1¼ **cups reduced-sodium chicken broth**

 1 **egg, lightly beaten**

*Jalapeño peppers can sting and irritate the skin, so wear rubber gloves when handling peppers and do not touch your eyes.

Note: For a more moist dressing, increase chicken broth to 1½ cups.

1. Trim excess fat from pork and discard. Coat large skillet with nonstick cooking spray; heat over medium heat until hot. Add pork; cook 10 minutes or until browned on both sides. Remove; set aside.

2. Add onion, celery, pecans, jalapeño, sage, rosemary and black pepper to skillet. Cook 5 minutes or until onion and celery are tender.

3. Combine cornbread stuffing mix, vegetable mixture and broth in medium bowl. Stir in egg. Spoon stuffing mixture into **CROCK-POT®** slow cooker. Arrange pork on top. Cover; cook on LOW about 5 hours or until pork is tender.

Makes 6 servings

Fall-Apart Pork Roast with Mole

²/₃ **cup whole almonds**

²/₃ **cup raisins**

3 **tablespoons vegetable oil, divided**

¹/₂ **cup chopped onion**

4 **cloves garlic, chopped**

2³/₄ **pounds lean boneless pork shoulder roast, well trimmed**

1 **can (14¹/₂ ounces) diced fire-roasted tomatoes or diced tomatoes, undrained**

1 **cup cubed bread, any variety**

¹/₂ **cup chicken broth**

2 **ounces Mexican chocolate, chopped**

2 **tablespoons chipotle peppers in adobo sauce, chopped**

1 **teaspoon salt**

Fresh cilantro, coarsely chopped (optional)

1. Heat large skillet over medium-high heat until hot. Add almonds and toast 3 to 4 minutes, stirring frequently, until fragrant. Add raisins. Cook 1 to 2 minutes longer, stirring constantly, until raisins begin to plump. Place half of almond mixture in large mixing bowl. Reserve remaining half for garnish.

2. In same skillet, heat 1 tablespoon oil. Add onion and garlic. Cook and stir 2 to 3 minutes until softened. Add to almond mixture; set aside.

3. Heat remaining oil in same skillet. Add pork roast and brown on all sides, about 5 to 7 minutes. Transfer to **CROCK-POT®** slow cooker.

4. Combine tomatoes with juice, bread, broth, chocolate, chipotle peppers and salt with almond mixture. Purée mixture in blender, in 2 to 3 batches, until smooth. Pour purée over pork roast in **CROCK-POT®** slow cooker. Cover; cook on LOW 7 to 8 hours or on HIGH 3 to 4 hours or until pork is done.

5. Remove pork roast from **CROCK-POT®** slow cooker. Whisk sauce until smooth before spooning over pork roast. Garnish with reserved almond mixture and chopped cilantro, if desired.

Makes 6 servings

Pork Loin Stuffed with Stone Fruits

1 **boneless pork loin roast (about 4 pounds)**

Salt and black pepper, to taste

2 **tablespoons vegetable oil**

2 **tablespoons butter**

1 **onion, chopped**

½ **cup Madeira or sherry wine**

1½ **cups dried stone fruits (½ cup each plums, peaches and apricots)**

2 **cloves garlic, minced**

¾ **teaspoon salt**

½ **teaspoon black pepper**

¼ **teaspoon dried thyme**

Kitchen string, cut into 15-inch lengths

1 **tablespoon olive oil**

Tip: To butterfly a roast means to split the meat down the center without cutting all the way through. This allows the meat to be spread open so a filling can be added.

1. Coat **CROCK-POT**® slow cooker with nonstick cooking spray. Season pork with salt and pepper. Heat vegetable oil in large skillet over medium-high heat until hot. Sear pork on all sides, turning as it browns. Transfer to cutting board; let stand until cool enough to handle.

2. Melt butter in same skillet over medium heat. Add onion. Cook and stir until translucent. Add Madeira. Cook 2 to 3 minutes until mixture reduces slightly. Stir in dried fruit, garlic, salt, pepper and thyme. Cook 1 minute longer. Remove skillet from heat.

3. Cut strings from roast, if any. Butterfly roast lengthwise (use sharp knife to cut meat; cut to within 1½ inches of edge). Spread roast flat on cutting board, browned side down. Spoon fruit mixture onto pork roast. Bring sides together to close roast. Slide kitchen string under roast and tie roast shut, allowing 2 inches between ties. If any fruit escapes, push back gently. Place roast in **CROCK-POT**® slow cooker. Pour olive oil over roast. Cover; cook on LOW 5 to 6 hours or on HIGH 2 to 3 hours, or until roast is tender.

4. Transfer roast to cutting board and let stand 10 minutes. Pour cooking liquid into small saucepan (strain through fine-mesh sieve first, if desired). Cook over high heat about 3 minutes to reduce sauce. Add salt and pepper to sauce, if desired. Slice roast and serve with sauce.

Makes 8 to 10 servings

Spicy Citrus Pork with Pineapple Salsa

1 **tablespoon ground cumin**

1/2 **teaspoon salt**

1 **teaspoon coarsely ground black pepper**

3 **pounds center-cut pork loin, rinsed and patted dry**

2 **tablespoons vegetable oil**

4 **cans (8 ounces each) pineapple tidbits* in own juice, drained, 1/2 cup juice reserved**

3 **tablespoons lemon juice, divided**

2 **teaspoons grated lemon peel**

1 **cup finely chopped orange or red bell pepper**

4 **tablespoons finely chopped red onion**

2 **tablespoons chopped fresh cilantro or mint**

1 **teaspoon grated fresh ginger (optional)**

1/4 **teaspoon red pepper flakes (optional)**

*If tidbits are unavailable, purchase pineapple chunks and coarsely chop.

Tip: If your pepper mill doesn't produce a coarse grind, you can place whole peppercorns in a plastic bag and use a rolling pin to crush and grind them neatly.

1. Coat **CROCK-POT®** slow cooker with nonstick cooking spray. Combine cumin, salt and pepper in small bowl. Rub evenly onto pork. Heat oil in medium skillet over medium-high heat until hot. Sear pork loin on all sides, turning as it browns, 1 to 2 minutes per side. Transfer to **CROCK-POT®** slow cooker.

2. Spoon 4 tablespoons of reserved pineapple juice and 2 tablespoons lemon juice over pork. Cover; cook on LOW 2 to 2 1/4 hours or on HIGH 1 hour and 10 minutes, or until meat is tender.

3. Meanwhile, combine pineapple, remaining 2 tablespoons pineapple juice, remaining 1 tablespoon lemon juice, lemon peel, bell pepper, onion, cilantro, ginger, if desired, and pepper flakes, if desired, in medium bowl. Toss gently and blend well; set aside.

4. Transfer pork to serving platter. Let pork stand 10 minutes before slicing. Arrange pork slices on serving platter. To serve, pour sauce evenly over slices. Serve salsa on side.

Makes 12 servings

Polska Kielbasa with Beer & Onions

¹/₃ **cup honey mustard**

¹/₃ **cup packed dark brown sugar**

18 **ounces brown ale or beer**

2 **kielbasa sausages (16 ounces each), cut into 4-inch pieces**

2 **onions, quartered**

Combine honey mustard and brown sugar in **CROCK-POT**® slow cooker. Whisk in ale. Add sausage pieces. Top with onions. Cover; cook on LOW 4 to 5 hours, stirring occasionally.

Makes 6 to 8 servings

Pecan and Apple Stuffed Pork Chops with Apple Brandy

4 **thick-cut, bone-in pork loin chops (about 12 ounces each)**

1 **teaspoon salt, divided**

¹/₂ **teaspoon black pepper, divided**

2 **tablespoons vegetable oil**

¹/₂ **cup diced green apple**

¹/₂ **small onion, minced**

¹/₄ **teaspoon dried thyme**

¹/₂ **cup apple brandy or brandy**

²/₃ **cup cubed white bread**

2 **tablespoons chopped pecans**

4 **tablespoons frozen butter**

1 **cup apple juice**

1. Coat **CROCK-POT**® slow cooker with nonstick cooking spray; set aside. Rinse pork chops and pat dry. Season with ¹/₂ teaspoon salt and ¹/₄ teaspoon pepper. Heat 2 tablespoons oil in large skillet over medium-high heat until hot. Sear pork chops about 2 minutes on both sides or until browned. Cook in 2 batches, if necessary; set aside.

2. Add apple, onion, thyme, remaining ¹/₂ teaspoon salt and remaining ¹/₄ teaspoon pepper to hot skillet and reduce heat to medium. Cook and stir 3 minutes or until onion is translucent. Remove from heat and pour in brandy. Return to medium heat and simmer until most of liquid is absorbed. Stir in bread and pecans, and cook 1 minute longer.

3. Cut each pork chop horizontally with sharp knife to form pocket. Place 1 tablespoon butter into each pocket. Divide stuffing among pork chops. Arrange pork chops in **CROCK-POT**® slow cooker, pocket side up.

4. Pour apple juice around pork chops. Cover; cook on HIGH 1¹/₂ to 1³/₄ hours or until pork is 155°F when measured with meat thermometer. (Do not overcook or pork chops will be dry.)

Makes 4 servings

Polska Kielbasa with Beer & Onions

Gingered Sherry Pork Roast

2 tablespoons extra-virgin olive oil

1 clove garlic, chopped

1 pork roast (about 2½ pounds)

12 baby carrots

12 baby red potatoes

6 petite onions

1 cup sherry

3 tablespoons hoisin sauce

1 tablespoon soy sauce

2 teaspoons grated fresh ginger

¼ teaspoon black pepper

2 tablespoons chopped fresh chives

Tip: Consider using your **CROCK-POT**® slow cooker as an extra "burner" that doesn't need watching. For example, you can cook this main dish in the **CROCK-POT**® slow cooker while you prepare the sides.

1. Heat oil in skillet over medium-high heat until hot. Add garlic. Cook and stir 30 seconds. Remove garlic with slotted spoon. Add pork roast and sear on all sides until golden brown, about 3 to 4 minutes per side. Remove roast; set aside.

2. Place carrots, potatoes and onions in **CROCK-POT**® slow cooker. Place seared pork roast on top of vegetables. Combine sherry, hoisin sauce, soy sauce, ginger and pepper in small bowl. Pour over roast. Cover; cook on LOW 6 to 8 hours or on HIGH 4 to 5 hours. Baste occasionally with sherry sauce.

3. Remove roast and let stand 10 minutes. Slice and return to **CROCK-POT**® slow cooker. Serve pork with vegetables and sauce. Garnish with chives.

Makes 4 servings

Cuban Pork Sandwiches

1 **pork loin roast (about 2 pounds)**

1/2 **cup orange juice**

2 **tablespoons lime juice**

1 **tablespoon minced garlic**

1 1/2 **teaspoons salt**

1/2 **teaspoon crushed red pepper flakes**

8 **crusty bread rolls, split in half (6 inches each)**

2 **tablespoons yellow mustard**

8 **slices Swiss cheese**

8 **thin ham slices**

4 **small dill pickles, thinly sliced lengthwise**

1. Coat **CROCK-POT®** slow cooker with nonstick cooking spray. Add pork loin.

2. Combine orange juice, lime juice, garlic, salt and red pepper flakes in small bowl. Pour over pork. Cover; cook on LOW 7 to 8 hours or on HIGH 3 1/2 to 4 hours. Transfer pork to cutting board and allow to cool. Cut into thin slices.

3. To serve, spread mustard on both sides of rolls. Divide pork slices among roll bottoms. Top with Swiss cheese slice, ham slice and pickle slices. Cover with top of roll.

4. Coat large skillet with nonstick cooking spray and heat over medium heat until hot. Working in batches, arrange sandwiches in skillet. Cover with foil and top with dinner plate to press down sandwiches. (If necessary, weight with 2 to 3 cans to compress sandwiches lightly.) Heat until cheese is slightly melted, about 8 minutes.* Serve immediately.

Makes 8 servings

*Or use tabletop grill to compress and heat sandwiches.

Fall-Off-the-Bone BBQ Ribs

½ **cup paprika**

⅜ **cup sugar**

¼ **cup onion powder**

1½ **teaspoons salt**

1½ **teaspoons black pepper**

2½ **pounds pork baby back ribs, silver skin removed**

1 **can (20 ounces) beer or beef stock**

1 **quart barbecue sauce**

½ **cup honey**

White sesame seeds and sliced chives (optional)

1. Preheat grill. Lightly oil grill grate.

2. While grill heats, combine paprika, sugar, onion powder, salt and pepper in large mixing bowl. Generously season ribs with dry rub mixture. Place ribs on grill. Cook for 3 minutes on each side or until ribs have grill marks.

3. Portion ribs into sections of 3 to 4 bones. Place in **CROCK-POT®** slow cooker. Pour beer over ribs. Cover; cook on HIGH 2 hours. Blend barbecue sauce and honey and add. Cover; cook 1½ hours longer. Garnish with white sesame seeds and chives, if desired. Serve with extra sauce on the side.

Makes 6 to 8 servings

Pork Roast Landaise

2 tablespoons olive oil

2½ pounds boneless, center-cut pork loin roast

Salt and black pepper, to taste

1 medium onion, diced

2 large cloves garlic, minced

2 teaspoons dried thyme

2 parsnips, cut into ¾-inch slices

¼ cup red wine vinegar

¼ cup sugar

½ cup port or sherry wine

2 cups chicken broth, divided

2 tablespoons cornstarch

3 pears, cored and sliced ¾ inch thick

1½ cups pitted prunes

1. Heat olive oil in large saucepan over medium-high heat. Season pork roast with salt and pepper; brown roast on all sides in saucepan. Place roast in **CROCK-POT**® slow cooker.

2. Add onion and garlic to saucepan. Cook and stir over medium heat 2 to 3 minutes. Stir in thyme. Transfer to **CROCK-POT**® slow cooker. Add parsnips; stir well.

3. Combine vinegar and sugar in same saucepan. Cook over medium heat, stirring constantly, until mixture thickens into syrup. Add port and cook 1 minute more. Add 1¾ cups chicken broth. Combine remaining ¼ cup of broth with cornstarch in small bowl. Whisk in cornstarch mixture, and cook until smooth and slightly thickened. Pour into **CROCK-POT**® slow cooker.

4. Cover; cook on LOW 8 hours or on HIGH 4 hours. Add pears and prunes during last 30 minutes of cooking.

Makes 4 to 6 servings

Lemon Pork Chops

1 **tablespoon vegetable oil**

4 **boneless pork chops**

3 **cans (8 ounces each) tomato sauce**

1 **large onion, quartered and sliced (optional)**

1 **large green bell pepper, cut into strips**

1 **tablespoon lemon-pepper seasoning**

1 **tablespoon Worcestershire sauce**

1 **large lemon, quartered**

Lemon wedges (optional)

Tip: Browning pork before adding it to the CROCK-POT® slow cooker helps reduce the fat. Just remember to drain off the fat in the skillet before transferring the pork to the CROCK-POT® slow cooker.

1. Heat oil in large skillet over medium-low heat until hot. Brown pork chops on both sides. Drain excess fat and discard. Transfer to **CROCK-POT®** slow cooker.

2. Combine tomato sauce, onion, if desired, bell pepper, lemon-pepper seasoning and Worcestershire sauce. Add to **CROCK-POT®** slow cooker.

3. Squeeze juice from lemon quarters over mixture; drop squeezed lemons into **CROCK-POT®** slow cooker. Cover; cook on LOW 6 to 8 hours or until pork is tender. Remove squeezed lemons before serving. Garnish with additional lemon wedges, if desired.

Makes 4 servings

**Pork
Entrées**

Pork Loin with Sherry and Red Onions

3 **large red onions, thinly sliced**

1 **cup pearl onions, blanched and peeled**

2 **tablespoons unsalted butter or margarine**

2½ **pounds boneless pork loin, tied**

½ **teaspoon salt**

½ **teaspoon ground black pepper**

½ **cup cooking sherry**

2 **tablespoons fresh chopped Italian parsley**

1½ **tablespoons cornstarch**

2 **tablespoons water**

Note: The mild flavor of pork is awakened by this rich, delectable sauce.

Tip: If using the 5-, 6- or 7-quart CROCK-POT® slow cooker, double all ingredients, except for the sherry, cornstarch and water.

1. Cook red and pearl onions in butter in medium skillet over medium heat until soft.

2. Rub pork loin with salt and pepper and place in **CROCK-POT®** slow cooker. Add cooked onions, sherry and parsley. Cover; cook on LOW 8 to 10 hours or on HIGH 5 to 6 hours.

3. Remove pork loin; cover and let stand 15 minutes before slicing.

4. Turn heat to HIGH. Combine cornstarch and water and stir into cooking liquid in **CROCK-POT®** slow cooker. Cook 15 minutes or until sauce has thickened. Serve sliced pork loin with onions and sherry sauce.

Makes 8 servings

Ham with Fruited Bourbon Sauce

1 bone-in ham, butt portion (about 6 pounds)

½ cup apple juice

¾ cup packed dark brown sugar

½ cup raisins

1 teaspoon ground cinnamon

¼ teaspoon red pepper flakes

⅓ cup dried cherries

¼ cup cornstarch

¼ cup bourbon, rum or apple juice

Tip: For easier cleanup of the CROCK-POT® slow cooker stoneware, spray the inside with nonstick cooking spray before adding ingredients.

1. Coat **CROCK-POT®** slow cooker with nonstick cooking spray. Add ham, cut-side up. Combine apple juice, brown sugar, raisins, cinnamon and red pepper flakes in small bowl; stir well. Pour mixture evenly over ham. Cover; cook on LOW 9 to 10 hours or on HIGH 4½ to 5 hours. Add cherries 30 minutes before end of cooking time.

2. Transfer ham to cutting board. Let stand 15 minutes before slicing.

3. Pour cooking liquid into large measuring cup and let stand 5 minutes. Skim and discard excess fat. Return cooking liquid to **CROCK-POT®** slow cooker.

4. Turn **CROCK-POT®** slow cooker to HIGH. Whisk cornstarch and bourbon in small bowl until cornstarch is dissolved. Stir into cooking liquid. Cover; cook on HIGH 15 to 20 minutes longer or until thickened. Serve sauce over sliced ham.

Makes 10 to 12 servings

Harvest Ham Supper

6 **carrots, cut into 2-inch pieces**

3 **medium sweet potatoes, quartered**

1 **to 1½ pounds boneless ham**

1 **cup maple syrup**

1. Arrange carrots and potatoes in bottom of **CROCK-POT®** slow cooker to form rack.

2. Place ham on top of vegetables. Pour syrup over ham and vegetables. Cover; cook on LOW 6 to 8 hours.

Makes 6 servings

Chinese Pork Tenderloin

2 **pork tenderloins (about 2 pounds total)**

1 **green bell pepper, seeded and cut into ½-inch dice**

1 **red bell pepper, seeded and cut into ½-inch dice**

1 **medium onion, thinly sliced**

2 **carrots, peeled and thinly sliced**

1 **jar (15 ounces) sweet and sour sauce**

1 **tablespoon soy sauce**

½ **teaspoon red pepper sauce**

Cooked white rice

Fresh cilantro or parsley (optional)

1. Cut pork into 1-inch cubes and place in **CROCK-POT®** slow cooker.

2. Add diced peppers, onion, carrots, sweet and sour sauce, soy sauce and red pepper sauce. Stir just to combine. Cover and cook on LOW 6 to 7 hours or on HIGH 4 to 5 hours. Stir again just before serving. Serve over hot rice and garnish with cilantro or parsley, if desired.

Makes 8 servings

Mediterranean Pepper Pot

1 pound mild Italian
sausage, removed from
casings

1½ cups water

1 can (15 ounces) navy
beans, rinsed and drained

¼ cup chopped pepperoncini
peppers*

1 medium yellow bell
pepper, cut into 1-inch
pieces

1 medium green bell pepper,
cut into 1-inch pieces

1 can (14½ ounces)
diced canned tomatoes,
undrained

2 teaspoons dried basil

1 teaspoon dried oregano

¼ cup ketchup

*Pepperoncini are pickled peppers
sold in jars with brine. They're
available in the supermarket
condiment aisle.

Tip: For an instant boost
in flavor, serve entrées
and main dishes made in
your **CROCK-POT®** slow
cooker with a garnish of
freshly grated cheese, such
as Parmesan, Romano or
Asiago.

1. Coat **CROCK-POT®** slow cooker with nonstick cooking spray.
Heat large skillet over medium-high heat until hot. Add sausage
and brown well. Drain and discard excess fat. Transfer to
CROCK-POT® slow cooker.

2. Add water, beans, peppers, tomatoes with juice, basil and
oregano. Cover; cook on LOW 7 to 8 hours or on HIGH 3 to
4 hours.

3. Add ketchup; stir well. Let stand, covered, 15 minutes before
serving.

Makes 4 servings

Sweet 'N' Spicy Ribs

5 cups barbecue sauce

¾ cup packed dark brown sugar

¼ cup honey

2 tablespoons Cajun seasoning

1 tablespoon garlic powder

1 tablespoon onion powder

6 pounds pork or beef back ribs, cut into 3-rib portions

Tip: To remove a small amount of fat from dishes cooked in the CROCK-POT® slow cooker, lightly pull a sheet of clean paper towel over the surface, letting the grease be absorbed by the paper towel. Repeat this process as necessary.

1. Combine barbecue sauce, sugar, honey, Cajun seasoning, garlic powder and onion powder in medium bowl. Remove 1 cup mixture; refrigerate and reserve for dipping sauce.

2. Place ribs in large **CROCK-POT®** slow cooker. Pour barbecue sauce mixture over ribs. Cover; cook on LOW 8 hours or until meat is very tender.

3. Transfer ribs to serving platter; cover with foil to keep warm. Skim fat from sauce and discard. Serve ribs with additional reserved sauce.

Makes 10 servings

Turkey Entrées

Harvest Time Turkey Meat Loaf

- **2 pounds ground turkey meat**
- **2 beaten eggs**
- **³/₄ cup bread crumbs**
- **1 apple, peeled, cored and coarsely grated**
- **¹/₄ cup apple juice**
- **¹/₄ cup minced onion**
- **¹/₂ cup shredded Cheddar cheese**
- **¹/₄ cup minced fresh parsley**
- **¹/₄ cup ground walnuts**
- **¹/₂ teaspoon ground allspice**
- **Parsley sprigs and cranberry sauce (optional)**

Combine all ingredients except parsley sprigs and cranberry sauce in large bowl. Mix well and shape into 7-inch round loaf. Place loaf in round **CROCK-POT®** slow cooker. Cover; cook on LOW 5 to 6 hours. Slice turkey and garnish with parsley and cranberry sauce, if desired.

Makes 6 servings

Turkey Paprikash

2 tablespoons all-purpose flour

¼ teaspoon salt, or to taste

¼ teaspoon black pepper, or to taste

¼ teaspoon sweet paprika

⅛ teaspoon crushed red pepper flakes

1 pound turkey tenderloins, cut lengthwise in half

2 tablespoons olive oil

1 small onion, chopped

1 clove garlic, minced

1 can (14½ ounces) diced tomatoes, undrained

12 ounces noodles

¼ cup sour cream

¼ cup pitted sliced green olives

Tip: Don't add water to the CROCK-POT® slow cooker unless the recipe specifically says to do so. Foods don't lose as much moisture during slow cooking as they do during conventional cooking, so follow recipe guidelines for best results.

1. Place flour, salt, pepper, paprika and red pepper flakes in resealable plastic food storage bag. Add turkey and shake well to coat. Heat oil in large skillet over medium-high heat until hot. Add turkey in single layer. Brown on all sides, about 3 minutes per side. Arrange turkey in single layer in **CROCK-POT®** slow cooker.

2. Add onion and garlic to skillet. Cook and stir over medium-high heat 2 minutes or until onion begins to turn golden. Transfer to **CROCK-POT®** slow cooker. Stir in tomatoes with juice. Cover; cook on LOW 1 to 2 hours or until turkey is tender.

3. Meanwhile, cook noodles until tender. Drain and place in large shallow bowl. Spoon turkey and sauce over noodles. Top with sour cream and olives.

Makes 4 servings

Braised Turkey Breasts with Lemon-Artichoke Heart Sauce

2 bone-in, skin-on turkey breast halves (about 2 pounds each)

2 teaspoons salt, plus additional for seasoning

¼ teaspoon black pepper, plus additional for seasoning

½ cup all-purpose flour

4 teaspoons vegetable oil, divided

4 large shallots, peeled and thinly sliced

½ cup dry sherry

1 lemon, sliced into ¼-inch-thick slices

2 tablespoons capers, rinsed and drained

4 thyme sprigs

1½ cups low-sodium chicken broth

2 cans (about 14 ounces each) artichoke hearts, drained

2 tablespoons finely chopped flat-leaf parsley

Hot cooked egg noodles (optional)

1. Season both sides of turkey breasts liberally with salt and pepper. Dredge in flour, shaking off excess. Warm 2 teaspoons oil in large skillet over medium-high heat. Add 1 turkey breast half, and cook until brown on both sides, about 4 minutes total. Transfer to **CROCK-POT**® slow cooker. Repeat with remaining 2 teaspoons oil and second turkey breast; transfer to **CROCK-POT**® slow cooker.

2. Reduce heat to medium and add shallots to skillet. Cook until softened and just beginning to brown, about 4 minutes. Add sherry and stir to scrape up browned bits from bottom of pan. Cook until pan is almost dry, about 30 seconds, then pour over turkey breasts. Add lemon slices, capers, thyme sprigs, 2 teaspoons salt and ¼ teaspoon pepper. Pour in chicken broth. Cover and cook on LOW 6 hours or until turkey breasts are tender and nearly falling off the bone.

3. Remove turkey breasts; set aside to cool 10 minutes. Remove and discard skin and bones.

4. Remove thyme from cooking liquid; discard. Skim fat from sauce. Stir in artichoke hearts and chopped parsley. Season to taste with salt and pepper. Slice turkey. Serve on hot cooked egg noodles, if desired, topped with Lemon-Artichoke Heart Sauce.

Makes 6 servings

Southwest Chipotle Turkey Sloppy Joe Hoagies

1 pound turkey Italian sausage, casings removed

1 bag (14 ounces) frozen green and red pepper strips with onions

1 can (6 ounces) tomato paste

1 tablespoon quick-cooking tapioca

1 tablespoon minced chipotle pepper in adobo sauce, plus 1 tablespoon sauce

2 teaspoons ground cumin

1/2 teaspoon dried thyme

4 hoagie rolls, split horizontally

1. Cook sausage in medium nonstick skillet over medium-high heat, stirring frequently to break up meat, until no longer pink. Transfer to **CROCK-POT**® slow cooker.

2. Stir in pepper strips, tomato paste, tapioca, chipotle and sauce, cumin and thyme. Cover and cook on LOW 8 to 10 hours. Serve on hoagie rolls.

Makes 4 servings

Lemon and Herb Turkey Breast

1 split turkey breast (about 3 pounds)

1/2 cup lemon juice

6 cloves garlic, minced

1/4 teaspoon dried parsley

1/4 teaspoon dried tarragon

1/4 teaspoon dried rosemary

1/4 teaspoon dried sage

1/4 teaspoon salt

1/4 teaspoon black pepper

1/2 cup dry white wine

1. Place turkey breast in **CROCK-POT**® slow cooker, adjusting turkey to fit as needed.

2. Combine remaining ingredients in small bowl. Pour over turkey breast. Cover; cook on LOW 8 to 10 hours or on HIGH 4 to 5 hours.

Makes 6 servings

Southwest Chipotle
Turkey Sloppy Joe
Hoagies

Cuban-Style Curried Turkey

4 tablespoons all-purpose flour

1 teaspoon salt, or to taste

½ teaspoon black pepper, or to taste

2 pounds turkey breast meat, cut into 1-inch cubes*

4 tablespoons vegetable oil, divided

2 small onions, chopped

2 cloves garlic, minced

2 cans (14½ ounces each) diced tomatoes, undrained

2 cans (15 ounces each) black beans, rinsed and drained

1 cup chicken broth

⅔ cup raisins

½ teaspoon curry powder

¼ teaspoon crushed red pepper flakes

Juice of 1 lime (2 tablespoons)

2 tablespoons minced fresh cilantro

2 tablespoons minced green onion (green part only)

4 cups cooked rice (optional)

*You may substitute turkey tenderloins; cut as directed.

Tip: Curry powder is a blend of different spices and can vary in spiciness from mild to quite hot. If you prefer a hotter flavor, look for Madras curry powder.

1. Combine flour, salt and pepper in resealable plastic food storage bag. Add turkey cubes and shake well to coat. Heat 2 tablespoons oil in large skillet over medium heat until hot. Add turkey and brown on all sides in batches, about 5 minutes per batch. Transfer to **CROCK-POT**® slow cooker.

2. Heat remaining 2 tablespoons oil in skillet. Add onions and cook and stir over medium heat 3 minutes or until golden. Stir in garlic and cook an additional 30 seconds. Transfer to **CROCK-POT**® slow cooker.

3. Stir in tomatoes with juice, beans, broth, raisins, curry powder and red pepper flakes. Cover; cook on LOW 1 hour. Stir in lime juice. Sprinkle with cilantro and green onion. Adjust seasonings, if desired. Serve over rice, if desired.

Makes 8 servings

Slow Cooker Turkey Breast

½ **to 1 teaspoon garlic
powder, or to taste**

½ **to 1 teaspoon paprika,
or to taste**

1 **turkey breast
(4 to 6 pounds)**

1 **tablespoon dried parsley
flakes, or to taste**

1. Blend garlic powder and paprika. Rub into turkey skin. Place turkey in **CROCK-POT**® slow cooker. Sprinkle on parsley. Cover; cook on LOW 6 to 8 hours or on HIGH 2½ to 3 hours or until internal temperature reaches 165°F when meat thermometer is inserted into thickest part of breast, not touching bone.

2. Transfer turkey to cutting board; cover with foil and let stand 10 to 15 minutes before carving. (Internal temperature will rise 5° to 10°F during stand time.)

Makes 4 to 6 servings

Turkey Scaloppini in Alfredo Sauce

2 **tablespoons all-purpose
flour**

¼ **teaspoon salt, or to taste**

¼ **teaspoon black pepper**

1 **pound turkey tenderloins,
cut lengthwise in half**

1 **tablespoon butter**

1 **tablespoon olive oil**

1 **cup refrigerated Alfredo
pasta sauce**

12 **ounces spinach noodles**

¼ **cup shredded Asiago or
Parmesan cheese**

1. Place flour, salt and pepper in resealable plastic food storage bag. Add turkey and shake well to coat. Heat butter and oil in large skillet over medium-high heat until hot. Add turkey in single layer. Brown on all sides, about 3 minutes per side. Arrange turkey in single layer in **CROCK-POT**® slow cooker.

2. Add Alfredo sauce. Cover; cook on LOW 1 to 1½ hours or until turkey is tender.

3. Meanwhile, cook noodles until tender. Drain and place in large shallow bowl. Spoon turkey and sauce over noodles. Garnish with cheese.

Makes 4 servings

**Slow Cooker
Turkey Breast**

Turkey with Chunky Cherry Relish

1 **bag (16 ounces) frozen dark cherries, coarsely chopped**

1 **can (about 14 ounces) diced tomatoes with jalapeños**

1 **package (6 ounces) dried cherry-flavored cranberries or dried cherries, coarsely chopped**

2 **small onions, thinly sliced**

1 **small green bell pepper, chopped**

½ **cup packed brown sugar**

2 **tablespoons tapioca**

1½ **tablespoons salt**

½ **teaspoon ground cinnamon**

½ **teaspoon black pepper**

1 **bone-in turkey breast (about 2½ to 3 pounds)**

2 **tablespoons water**

1 **tablespoon cornstarch**

1. Place cherries, tomatoes, cranberries, onions, bell pepper, brown sugar, tapioca, salt, cinnamon and black pepper in **CROCK-POT®** slow cooker; mix well.

2. Place turkey on top of mixture. Cover; cook on LOW 7 to 8 hours or until temperature registers over 170°F on meat thermometer inserted into thickest part of breast, not touching bone. Remove turkey from **CROCK-POT®** slow cooker; keep warm.

3. Increase temperature to HIGH. Combine water and cornstarch in small bowl to form smooth paste. Stir into cherry mixture. Cook, uncovered, on HIGH 15 minutes or until sauce is thickened. Adjust seasonings, if desired. Slice turkey and top with relish.

Makes 4 to 6 servings

Tarragon Turkey and Pasta

1½ to 2 pounds turkey tenderloins

½ cup thinly sliced celery

¼ cup thinly sliced green onions

4 tablespoons fresh tarragon, minced

¼ cup dry white wine

1 teaspoon salt

1 teaspoon freshly ground black pepper

½ cup plain yogurt

1 tablespoon fresh minced Italian parsley

1 tablespoon lemon juice

1½ tablespoons cornstarch

2 tablespoons water

4 cups pasta of your choice, cooked al denté

Tip: Recipe can be doubled for a 5-, 6- or 7-quart CROCK-POT® slow cooker.

1. Combine turkey, celery, green onions, 2 tablespoons fresh tarragon, wine, salt and pepper in **CROCK-POT®** slow cooker. Mix thoroughly. Cover; cook on LOW 6 to 8 hours or on HIGH 3½ to 4 hours or until turkey is no longer pink.

2. Remove turkey; cut into ½-inch-thick medallions. Turn **CROCK-POT®** slow cooker to HIGH. Stir yogurt, remaining 2 tablespoons fresh tarragon, parsley and lemon juice into cooking liquid.

3. Combine cornstarch and water in small bowl. Stir into cooking liquid and cook until thickened. Serve turkey medallions over pasta. Drizzle with tarragon sauce.

Makes 4 servings

Saucy Tropical Turkey

3 **to 4 turkey thighs
(about 2½ pounds),
skin removed**

2 **tablespoons vegetable oil**

1 **small onion, sliced**

1 **can (20 ounces) pineapple
chunks, drained**

1 **red bell pepper, cubed**

²/₃ **cup apricot preserves**

3 **tablespoons soy sauce**

1 **teaspoon grated lemon
peel**

1 **teaspoon ground ginger**

¼ **cup cold water**

2 **tablespoons cornstarch**

Hot cooked rice

**Tip: Recipes often provide
a range of cooking times to
account for variables, such
as the temperature of the
ingredients before cooking,
the quantity of food in your
CROCK-POT® slow cooker
and the altitude; cooking
times will be longer at
higher altitudes.**

1. Rinse turkey and pat dry. Heat oil in large skillet over medium-high heat until hot. Brown turkey on all sides. Place onion in **CROCK-POT®** slow cooker. Transfer turkey to **CROCK-POT®** slow cooker; top with pineapple and bell pepper.

2. Combine preserves, soy sauce, lemon peel and ginger in small bowl; mix well. Spoon over turkey. Cover; cook on LOW 6 to 7 hours.

3. Transfer turkey to serving platter; cover with foil to keep warm. Blend water and cornstarch until smooth; stir into cooking liquid. Cook, uncovered, on HIGH 15 minutes or until sauce is slightly thickened. Adjust seasonings, if necessary. Return turkey to **CROCK-POT®** slow cooker; cook until hot. Serve with rice.

Makes 6 servings

Spicy Turkey with Citrus au Jus

1 **bone-in turkey breast, thawed, rinsed and patted dry (about 4 pounds)**

¼ **cup (½ stick) butter, at room temperature**

Grated peel of 1 medium lemon

1 **teaspoon chili powder**

¼ **to ½ teaspoon black pepper**

⅛ **to ¼ teaspoon red pepper flakes**

1 **tablespoon lemon juice**

Salt and black pepper (optional)

1. Coat **CROCK-POT**® slow cooker with nonstick cooking spray. Add turkey breast.

2. Mix butter, lemon peel, chili powder, black pepper and red pepper flakes in small bowl until well blended. Spread mixture over top and sides of turkey. Cover; cook on LOW 4 to 5 hours or on HIGH 2½ to 3 hours or until meat thermometer reaches 165°F and juices run clear. Do not overcook.

3. Transfer turkey to cutting board. Let stand 10 minutes before slicing. Turn **CROCK-POT**® slow cooker to LOW.

4. Stir lemon juice into cooking liquid. Pour mixture through fine-mesh sieve; discard solids in sieve. Let mixture stand 5 minutes. Skim and discard excess fat. Add salt and pepper, if desired. Return au jus mixture to **CROCK-POT**® slow cooker. Cover to keep warm. Serve au jus with turkey.

Makes 6 to 8 servings

Turkey Breast with Barley-Cranberry Stuffing

2 cups reduced-sodium chicken broth

1 cup uncooked quick-cooking barley

½ cup chopped onion

½ cup dried cranberries

2 tablespoons slivered almonds, toasted*

½ teaspoon rubbed sage

½ teaspoon garlic-pepper seasoning

1 fresh or thawed frozen bone-in turkey breast half (about 2 pounds), skinned

⅓ cup finely chopped fresh parsley

*To toast almonds, spread in single layer on baking sheet. Bake in preheated 350°F oven 8 to 10 minutes or until golden brown, stirring frequently.

Tip: Browning poultry before cooking it in the CROCK-POT® slow cooker isn't necessary but helps to enhance the flavor and adds an oven-roasted appearance to the finished dish.

1. Thaw turkey breast, if frozen. Remove skin and discard.

2. Combine broth, barley, onion, cranberries, almonds, sage and garlic-pepper seasoning in **CROCK-POT®** slow cooker.

3. Coat large nonstick skillet with cooking spray. Heat over medium heat until hot. Brown turkey breast on all sides; add to **CROCK-POT®** slow cooker. Cover; cook on LOW 4 to 6 hours.

4. Transfer turkey to cutting board; cover with foil to keep warm. Let stand 10 to 15 minutes before carving. Stir parsley into sauce mixture in **CROCK-POT®** slow cooker. Serve over sliced turkey and stuffing.

Makes 6 servings

Turkey Piccata

2½ tablespoons all-purpose flour

¼ teaspoon salt, or to taste

¼ teaspoon black pepper

1 pound turkey breast meat, cut into short strips*

1 tablespoon butter

1 tablespoon olive oil

½ cup chicken broth

2 teaspoons freshly squeezed lemon juice

Grated peel of 1 lemon

2 tablespoons finely chopped parsley

2 cups cooked rice (optional)

*You may substitute turkey tenderloins; cut as directed.

Tip: This recipe will also work with chicken strips. Start with boneless, skinless chicken breasts, then follow the recipe as directed.

1. Combine flour, salt and pepper in resealable plastic food storage bag. Add turkey strips and shake well to coat. Heat butter and oil in large skillet over medium-high heat until hot. Add turkey strips in single layer. Brown on all sides, about 2 minutes per side. Transfer to **CROCK-POT®** slow cooker, arranging on bottom in single layer.

2. Pour broth into skillet. Cook and stir to scrape up any browned bits. Pour into **CROCK-POT®** slow cooker. Add lemon juice and peel. Cover; cook on LOW 1 hour. Sprinkle with parsley before serving. Serve over rice, if desired.

Makes 4 servings

Vegetarian Entrées

Vegetable Paella

2 tablespoons olive oil
1 medium onion, chopped
1 medium red bell pepper, seeded and ribbed, chopped
2 cloves garlic, minced
1½ cups converted rice
2 cans (14½ ounces each) vegetable broth
½ cup dry white wine
½ teaspoon crushed saffron threads, smoked paprika, or ground turmeric
¾ teaspoon salt
¼ teaspoon red pepper flakes
1 can (about 15 ounces) garbanzo beans (drained and rinsed)
1 package (11 ounces) frozen artichoke hearts, thawed
½ cup frozen peas, thawed

1. Heat oil in medium skillet over medium heat. Add onion, bell pepper and garlic. Cook, stirring occasionally until onion softens. Transfer to **CROCK-POT**® slow cooker. Add rice, broth, wine, saffron, salt and red pepper flakes. Stir to level rice. Cover; cook on LOW 3 hours.

2. Add garbanzo beans, artichoke hearts and peas to **CROCK-POT**® slow cooker; do not stir. Cover and cook on LOW about 30 minutes, until rice is tender and liquid is absorbed. Stir well and serve hot.

Makes 6 servings

Vegetarian Entrées

Asian Sweet Potato and Corn Stew

1 tablespoon vegetable oil

1 large onion, chopped

2 tablespoons peeled and minced fresh ginger

½ jalapeño or serrano pepper, seeded and minced*

2 cloves garlic, minced

1 cup drained canned or thawed frozen corn kernels

2 teaspoons curry powder

1 can (13½ ounces) coconut milk, well shaken

1 teaspoon cornstarch

1 can (14½ ounces) vegetable broth

1 tablespoon soy sauce, plus more to taste

4 sweet potatoes, peeled and cut into ¾-inch cubes

Hot cooked jasmine or long-grain rice

Chopped cilantro (optional)

*Jalapeño and serrano peppers can sting and irritate the skin, so wear rubber gloves when handling peppers and do not touch your eyes.

Tip: Garnish with coarsely chopped dry-roasted peanuts and chopped green onions for extra flavor and crunch.

1. Heat oil in large skillet over medium heat. Add onion, ginger, minced jalapeño and garlic. Cook, stirring occasionally, until onion softens (about 5 minutes). Remove from heat and stir in drained corn and curry powder.

2. Whisk coconut milk and cornstarch together in **CROCK-POT®** slow cooker. Stir in broth and soy sauce. Carefully add sweet potatoes then top with curried corn. Cover; cook on LOW 5 to 6 hours or until sweet potatoes are tender. Stir gently to smooth cooking liquid (coconut milk may look curdled) without breaking up sweet potatoes. Adjust seasoning to taste with additional soy sauce. Spoon over rice in serving bowls and sprinkle with cilantro, if desired.

Makes 6 servings

Black Bean and Mushroom Chilaquiles

2 tablespoons olive oil

1 medium onion, chopped

1 medium green bell pepper, seeded and ribbed, chopped

1 jalapeño or serrano pepper, seeded and minced*

2 cans (about 15 ounces each) black beans, drained and rinsed

1 can (14½ ounces) diced tomatoes, undrained

10 ounces white mushrooms, cut into quarters

1½ teaspoons ground cumin

1½ teaspoons dried oregano

1 cup (about 2 ounces) shredded sharp white Cheddar cheese, plus additional cheese for garnish

6 cups baked tortilla chips

*Jalapeño and serrano peppers can sting and irritate the skin, so wear rubber gloves when handling peppers and do not touch your eyes.

1. Heat oil in medium skillet over medium heat. Add onion, bell pepper and minced jalapeño. Cook, stirring occasionally, until onion softens. Transfer to **CROCK-POT**® slow cooker. Add beans, tomatoes with juice, mushrooms, cumin and oregano. Cover; cook on LOW 6 hours or on HIGH 3 hours.

2. Remove cover and sprinkle Cheddar cheese over beans and mushrooms. Cover again and cook until cheese melts; stir to combine melted cheese.

3. For each serving, coarsely crush 1 cup tortilla chips in individual serving bowl. Top with black bean mixture, sprinkle with additional cheese (if desired) and serve.

Makes 6 servings

Vegetable Jollof Rice

1 medium eggplant (about 1¼ pounds), trimmed and cut into 1-inch cubes

1¾ teaspoons salt, divided

3 tablespoons vegetable oil, plus more as needed

1 medium onion, chopped

1 medium green bell pepper, seeded and chopped

3 medium carrots, cut into ½-inch-thick rounds

2 cloves garlic, minced

1½ cups converted rice

1 tablespoon plus ½ teaspoon chili powder

1 can (28 ounces) diced tomatoes in juice, undrained

1 can (14½ ounces) vegetable broth

Tip: Jollof Rice (also spelled "jolof" or sometimes "djolof") is an important dish in many West African cultures.

1. Place eggplant cubes in colander. Toss with 1 teaspoon salt. Let stand in sink for 1 hour to drain. Rinse under cold water, drain and pat dry with paper towels.

2. Heat 1 tablespoon oil in large skillet over medium-high heat. Working in batches, add eggplant to skillet and cook turning to brown on all sides. Remove eggplant to plate as it is browned. Add additional oil, 1 tablespoon at a time, to skillet as needed to prepare all remaining batches of eggplant.

3. Wipe out skillet with paper towels. Add another 1 tablespoon oil to skillet and heat. Add onion, bell pepper, carrots and garlic. Cook, stirring occasionally, until onion is soft but not brown. Add to **CROCK-POT®** slow cooker. Stir in rice, chili powder and ¾ teaspoon salt.

4. Drain tomatoes over 1-quart measuring cup, reserving tomato juice. Add vegetable broth to tomato juice. Add additional water as needed to measure 4 cups total. Pour into **CROCK-POT®** slow cooker. Add drained tomatoes and stir to level rice; top with eggplant. Cover; cook on LOW 3½ to 4 hours or until rice is tender and liquid is absorbed. Stir well and serve hot.

Makes 6 servings

Curried Potatoes, Cauliflower and Peas

1 tablespoon vegetable oil

1 large onion, chopped

2 tablespoons peeled and minced fresh ginger

2 cloves garlic, chopped

2 pounds red-skinned potatoes, scrubbed, cut into 1/2-inch-thick rounds

1 teaspoon garam masala*

1 teaspoon salt, plus more to taste

1 small (about 1¼ pounds) head cauliflower, trimmed and broken into florets

1 cup canned vegetable broth or water

2 ripe plum (Roma) tomatoes, seeded and chopped

1 cup thawed frozen peas

Hot cooked basmati or long-grain rice

*Garam masala is a blend of Asian spices available in the spice aisle of many supermarkets. If garam masala is unavailable substitute 1/2 teaspoon ground cumin and 1/2 teaspoon ground coriander seeds.

1. Heat oil in large skillet over medium heat. Add onion, ginger and garlic. Cook, stirring occasionally, until onion softens. Remove from heat and set aside.

2. Put potatoes in **CROCK-POT**® slow cooker. Mix garam masala and salt in small bowl. Sprinkle half of spice mixture over potatoes. Top with onion mixture, then cauliflower. Sprinkle remaining spice mixture over cauliflower. Pour in broth. Cover; cook on HIGH 3½ hours.

3. Remove cover and gently stir in tomatoes and peas. Cover and cook for 30 minutes more or until potatoes are tender. Stir gently. Adjust seasoning with more salt, if desired. Spoon over rice in bowls and serve.

Makes 6 servings

Vegetarian Entrées

Three-Bean Chipotle Chili

2 tablespoons olive oil

1 large onion, chopped

1 medium green bell pepper, seeded, ribbed, and chopped

2 cloves garlic, minced

1 or 2 canned chipotles in adobo sauce, finely chopped

1 can (6 ounces) tomato paste

1 cup water

2 cans (about 15 ounces) pinto or pink beans, drained and rinsed

1 can (about 15 ounces) small white beans, drained and rinsed

1 can (about 15 ounces) garbanzo beans

1 cup drained canned or thawed frozen corn

Salt

Sour cream (optional)

Shredded Cheddar cheese (optional)

Chopped onion (optional)

1. Heat oil in large skillet over medium heat. Add onion, green pepper and garlic. Cook, stirring occasionally, until onion softens. Transfer to **CROCK-POT®** slow cooker.

2. Stir in chipotle peppers, tomato paste and water. Add pinto, white and garbanzo beans and corn. Cover; cook on LOW 3½ to 4 hours. Season to taste with salt. Garnish as desired with sour cream, shredded Cheddar cheese and chopped onion.

Makes 6 servings

Italian Escarole and White Bean Stew

1 **tablespoon olive oil**

1 **medium onion, chopped**

3 **medium carrots, cut into
½-inch-thick rounds**

2 **cloves garlic, minced**

1 **head (about 12 ounces)
escarole**

2 **cans (15½ ounces each)
Great Nothern white
beans**

1 **cans (14½ ounces each)
vegetable broth**

¼ **teaspoon red pepper
flakes**

 Salt, to taste

 **Grated Parmesan cheese
(optional)**

**Note: Escarole is very leafy
and easily fills a 4½-quart
CROCK-POT® slow cooker
when raw, but it shrinks
dramatically as it cooks
down. This recipe makes
4 portions, but can easily
be doubled. Simply double
the quantities of all the
ingredients listed and be
sure to use a 6-quart (or
larger) CROCK-POT® slow
cooker.**

1. Heat oil in medium skillet over medium-high heat. Add onion and carrots. Cook, stirring occasionally, until onion softens. Add garlic and stir until fragrant, about 1 minute. Transfer to **CROCK-POT**® slow cooker. Top with vegetable broth.

2. Trim off base of escarole. Roughly cut crosswise into 1-inch wide strips. Wash well in large bowl of cold water. Lift out by handfuls, leaving sand or dirt in bottom of bowl. Shake to remove excess water, but do not dry. Add to vegetable mixture in **CROCK-POT**® slow cooker. Sprinkle with red pepper flakes. Top with beans.

3. Cover; cook on LOW 7 to 8 hours or on HIGH 3½ to 4 hours, until escarole is wilted and very tender. Season with salt. Serve in bowls and sprinkle with Parmesan cheese, if desired.

Makes 4 servings

Ratatouille with Garbanzo Beans

3 tablespoons olive oil, divided

4 cloves garlic, minced

1 yellow onion, cut into ½-inch dice

4 small Italian eggplants, peeled and cut into ¾- to 1-inch dice

Salt and black pepper, to taste

1 red bell pepper, seeded and cut into ¾- to 1-inch dice

1 yellow bell pepper, seeded and cut into ¾- to 1-inch dice

1 orange bell pepper, seeded and cut into ¾- to 1-inch dice

3 small zucchini, cut into ¾-inch dice

1 can (15 to 20 ounces) garbanzo beans, rinsed and drained

2 cups crushed tomatoes

¼ cup fresh basil

2 tablespoons chopped fresh thyme

½ to 1 teaspoon crushed red pepper flakes

Fresh basil (optional)

1. Heat 1 tablespoon oil in skillet on medium-low until hot. Add garlic and onion, and cook 2 to 3 minutes or until translucent. Add eggplants, season with salt and black pepper and cook 1 to 2 minutes. Turn heat to low and cover. Cook 4 to 5 minutes, or until eggplants are tender. Transfer to **CROCK-POT®** slow cooker.

2. Add bell peppers, zucchini and garbanzo beans.

3. Combine tomatoes, basil, thyme, red pepper flakes and remaining 2 tablespoons oil in medium bowl; stir well. Pour into **CROCK-POT®** slow cooker. Stir together all ingredients.

4. Cover; cook on LOW 7 to 8 hours or on HIGH 4½ to 5 hours, or until vegetables are tender. Adjust seasonings. Garnish with fresh basil, if desired.

Makes 6 to 8 servings

Bean and Vegetable Burritos

2 tablespoons chili powder

2 teaspoons dried oregano

1½ teaspoons ground cumin

1 large sweet potato, peeled and diced

1 can (15 ounces) black beans, rinsed and drained

4 cloves garlic, minced

1 medium onion, halved and thinly sliced

1 jalapeño pepper, seeded and minced*

1 green bell pepper, chopped

1 cup frozen corn, thawed and drained

3 tablespoons lime juice

1 tablespoon chopped fresh cilantro

¾ cup (3 ounces) shredded Monterey Jack cheese

4 (10-inch) flour tortillas

*Jalapeño peppers can sting and irritate the skin, so wear rubber gloves when handling peppers and do not touch your eyes.

1. Combine chili powder, oregano and cumin in small bowl. Set aside.

2. Layer ingredients in **CROCK-POT®** slow cooker in following order: sweet potato, beans, half of chili powder mixture, garlic, onion, jalapeño pepper, bell pepper, remaining half of chili powder mixture and corn. Cover; cook on LOW 5 hours or until sweet potato is tender. Stir in lime juice and cilantro.

3. Preheat oven to 350°F. Spoon 2 tablespoons cheese into center of each tortilla. Top with 1 cup filling. Fold up bottom edge of tortilla over filling; fold in sides and roll to enclose filling. Place burrito, seam-side down, on baking sheet. Repeat with remaining tortillas. Cover with foil and bake 20 to 30 minutes or until heated through.

Makes 4 servings

Black Bean Stuffed Peppers

1 **medium onion, finely chopped**

Nonstick cooking spray

¼ **teaspoon ground red pepper**

¼ **teaspoon dried oregano**

¼ **teaspoon ground cumin**

¼ **teaspoon chili powder**

1 **can (15 ounces) black beans, rinsed and drained**

6 **tall green bell peppers, tops removed, seeded and cored**

1 **cup (4 ounces) shredded reduced-fat Monterey Jack cheese**

1 **cup tomato salsa**

½ **cup fat-free sour cream**

Snipped chives (optional)

Tip: You may increase any of the recipe ingredients to taste except the tomato soup, and use a 5-, 6- or 7-quart CROCK-POT® slow cooker. However, the peppers should fit comfortably in a single layer in your stoneware.

1. Cook onion in medium skillet, sprayed with cooking spray, until golden. Add the ground red pepper, oregano, cumin and chili powder.

2. Mash half of black beans with cooked onion in medium bowl. Stir in remaining beans. Place bell peppers in **CROCK-POT®** slow cooker; spoon black bean mixture into bell peppers. Sprinkle cheese over peppers. Pour salsa over cheese. Cover; cook on LOW 6 to 8 hours or on HIGH 3 to 4 hours.

3. Serve each pepper with a dollop of sour cream. Garnish with snipped chives, if desired

Makes 6 servings

Pasta, Potato and Rice Sides

Spinach Risotto

2 teaspoons butter

2 teaspoons olive oil

3 tablespoons finely chopped shallot

1¼ cups Arborio rice

½ cup dry white wine

3 cups chicken broth

½ teaspoon coarse salt

2 cups baby spinach

¼ cup grated Parmesan cheese

2 tablespoons pine nuts, toasted

1. Melt butter in medium skillet over medium heat; add olive oil. Add shallot and cook, stirring frequently, until softened but not browned.

2. Stir in rice and cook 2 to 3 minutes or until chalky and well coated. Stir in wine and cook until reduced by half. Transfer to **CROCK-POT®** slow cooker. Stir in broth and salt.

3. Cover and cook on HIGH 2 to 2½ hours or until rice is almost cooked but still contains a little liquid. Stir in spinach. Cover and cook 15 to 20 minutes or until spinach is cooked and and rice is tender and creamy. Gently stir in Parmesan cheese and pine nuts just before serving.

Makes 4 servings

Wild Rice with Fruit & Nuts

2 cups wild rice (or wild rice blend), rinsed*

½ cup dried cranberries

½ cup chopped raisins

½ cup chopped dried apricots

½ cup almond slivers, toasted**

5 to 6 cups chicken broth

1 cup orange juice

2 tablespoons butter, melted

1 teaspoon ground cumin

2 green onions, thinly sliced

2 to 3 tablespoons chopped fresh parsley

Salt and black pepper

*Do not use parboiled rice or a blend containing parboiled rice.

**To toast almonds, spread in single layer in heavy-bottomed skillet. Cook over medium heat 1 to 2 minutes, stirring frequently, until nuts are lightly browned. Remove from skillet immediately. Cool before using.

1. Combine wild rice, cranberries, raisins, apricots and almonds in **CROCK-POT**® slow cooker.

2. Combine broth, orange juice, butter and cumin in medium bowl. Pour mixture over rice and stir to mix.

3. Cover; cook on LOW 7 hours or on HIGH 2½ to 3 hours. Stir once, adding more hot broth if necessary.

4. When rice is soft, add green onions and parsley. Adjust seasoning to taste with salt and pepper, if desired. Cook 10 minutes longer and serve.

Makes 6 to 8 servings

Asiago and Asparagus Risotto-Style Rice

- **2 cups chopped onion**
- **1 cup uncooked converted rice**
- **2 medium cloves garlic, minced**
- **1 can (14½ ounces) chicken broth**
- **½ pound asparagus spears, trimmed and broken into 1-inch pieces**
- **1 to 1¼ cups half-and-half, divided**
- **½ cup (about 4 ounces) shredded Asiago cheese, plus more for garnish**
- **¼ cup (½ stick) butter, cut into small pieces**
- **2 ounces pine nuts or slivered almonds, toasted**
- **1 teaspoon salt**

1. Combine onion, rice, garlic and broth in **CROCK-POT®** slow cooker. Stir until well blended; cover and cook 2 hours on HIGH or until rice is done.

2. Stir in asparagus and ½ cup half-and-half. Cover and cook 20 to 30 minutes more or until asparagus is just tender.

3. Stir in remaining ingredients, then cover and let stand 5 minutes to allow cheese to melt slightly. Fluff with fork and garnish with additional Asiago cheese, if desired, before serving.

Makes 4 servings

Tip: Risotto is a classic creamy rice dish of northern Italy. It can be made with a wide variety of ingredients; fresh vegetables and cheeses such as Asiago work especially well in risottos. Parmesan cheese, shellfish, white wine and herbs are also popular additions.

Wild Rice and Dried Cherry Risotto

1 cup dry-roasted salted peanuts

2 tablespoons sesame oil, divided

1 cup chopped onion

6 ounces uncooked wild rice

1 cup diced carrot

1 cup chopped green or red bell pepper

½ cup dried cherries

⅛ to **¼** teaspoon red pepper flakes

4 cups hot water

¼ cup teriyaki or soy sauce

1 teaspoon salt, or to taste

1. Coat **CROCK-POT**® slow cooker with nonstick cooking spray. Heat large skillet over medium-high heat until hot. Add peanuts. Cook and stir 2 to 3 minutes or until peanuts begin to brown. Transfer peanuts to plate; set aside.

2. Heat 2 teaspoons sesame oil in skillet until hot. Add onion. Cook and stir 6 minutes or until richly browned. Transfer to **CROCK-POT**® slow cooker.

3. Stir in wild rice, carrot, bell pepper, cherries, red pepper flakes and water. Cover; cook on HIGH 3 hours.

4. Let stand 15 minutes, uncovered, until rice absorbs liquid. Stir in teriyaki sauce, peanuts, remaining oil and salt.

Makes 8 to 10 servings

Artichoke and Tomato Paella

4 cups vegetable broth

2 cups converted white rice

5 ounces (½ 10-ounce package) frozen chopped spinach, thawed and drained

1 green bell pepper, cored, seeded and chopped

1 medium ripe tomato, sliced into wedges

1 medium yellow onion, chopped

1 medium carrot, peeled and diced

3 cloves garlic, minced

1 tablespoon minced flat-leaf parsley

1 teaspoon salt

½ teaspoon black pepper

1 can (13¾ ounces) artichoke hearts, quartered, rinsed and well-drained

½ cup frozen peas

1. Combine broth, rice, spinach, bell pepper, tomato, onion, carrot, garlic, parsley, salt and black pepper in **CROCK-POT®** slow cooker. Mix thoroughly. Cover; cook on LOW 4 hours or on HIGH 2 hours.

2. Before serving, add artichoke hearts and peas. Cover; cook on HIGH 15 minutes. Mix well before serving.

Makes 8 servings

Cuban Black Beans and Rice

3¾ cups chicken broth

1½ cups uncooked brown rice

1 large onion, chopped

1 jalapeño pepper, seeded and chopped*

3 cloves garlic, minced

2 teaspoons ground cumin

1 teaspoon salt

2 cans (15 ounces each) black beans, rinsed and drained

1 tablespoon fresh lime juice

Sour cream (optional)

Chopped green onions (optional)

*Jalapeño peppers can sting and irritate the skin, so wear rubber gloves when handling peppers and do not touch your eyes.

1. Place chicken broth, rice, onion, jalapeño pepper, garlic, cumin and salt in **CROCK-POT**® slow cooker, mixing well. Cover and cook on LOW 7½ hours or until rice is tender.

2. Stir in beans and lime juice. Cover and cook 15 to 20 minutes more or until beans are heated through. Garnish with sour cream and green onions, if desired.

Makes 4 to 6 servings

Mediterranean Red Potatoes

3 medium red potatoes,
cut into bite-size pieces

²/₃ cup fresh or frozen pearl
onions

Garlic-flavored cooking
spray

¾ teaspoon dried Italian
seasoning

¼ teaspoon black pepper

1 small tomato, seeded and
chopped

2 ounces (¹/₂ cup) feta
cheese, crumbled

2 tablespoons chopped
black olives

1. Place potatoes and onions in 1¹/₂-quart soufflé dish. Spray with cooking spray; toss to coat. Add Italian seasoning and pepper; mix well. Cover dish tightly with foil.

2. Tear off 3 (18 × 3-inch) strips of heavy-duty foil. Cross strips to resemble wheel spokes. Place soufflé dish in center of strips. Pull foil strips up and over dish and place dish into **CROCK-POT®** slow cooker.

3. Pour hot water into **CROCK-POT®** slow cooker to about 1¹/₂ inches from top of soufflé dish. Cover; cook on LOW 7 to 8 hours.

4. Use foil handles to lift dish out of **CROCK-POT®** slow cooker. Stir chopped tomato, feta cheese and olives into potato mixture.

Makes 4 servings

Ziti Ratatouille

1 **large eggplant, peeled
and cut into** $1/2$**-inch cubes
(about 1**$1/2$ **pounds)**

2 **medium zucchini, cut into
$1/2$-inch cubes**

1 **green or red bell pepper,
seeded and cut into
$1/2$-inch pieces**

1 **large onion, chopped**

4 **cloves garlic, minced**

1 **jar (about 24 ounces)
marinara sauce**

2 **cans (about 14 ounces
each) diced tomatoes
with garlic and onions,
undrained**

1 **can (6 ounces) pitted
black olives, drained**

1 **package (8 ounces) ziti
noodles**

Lemon juice (optional)

**Shredded Parmesan
cheese (optional)**

1. Combine eggplant, zucchini, bell pepper, onion, garlic, marinara sauce, tomatoes with juices and black olives in **CROCK-POT**® slow cooker. Cover and cook on LOW 4$1/2$ hours.

2. Stir in pasta and cook 25 minutes more. drizzle with lemon juice and sprinkle with Parmesan cheese, if desired.

Makes 6 to 8 servings

Simmered Red Beans with Rice

2 cans (about 15 ounces each) red beans, rinsed and drained

1 can (about 14 ounces) diced tomatoes, undrained

½ cup chopped celery

½ cup chopped green bell pepper

½ cup chopped green onions with tops

2 cloves garlic, minced

1 to 2 teaspoons hot pepper sauce

1 teaspoon Worcestershire sauce

1 bay leaf

Hot cooked rice

1. Combine all ingredients except rice in **CROCK-POT**® slow cooker. Cover; cook on LOW 4 to 6 hours or on HIGH 2 to 3 hours.

2. Slightly mash mixture with potato masher to thicken. Continue to cook on LOW 30 to 60 minutes. Serve over rice.

Makes 6 servings

Coconut-Lime Scented Sweet Potatoes with Walnuts

2½ **pounds sweet potatoes, peeled and cut into 1-inch pieces**

8 **ounces shredded, peeled carrots**

¾ **cup sweetened coconut flakes, divided**

¼ **cup (½ stick) butter, melted**

3 **tablespoons sugar**

½ **teaspoon salt**

¾ **cup walnuts, toasted and coarsely chopped, divided**

2 **teaspoons grated lime peel**

1. Combine sweet potatoes, carrots, ½ cup coconut flakes, butter, sugar and salt in **CROCK-POT®** slow cooker. Cover and cook on LOW 5 to 6 hours, until sweet potatoes are tender and cooked through.

2. Meanwhile, add remaining ¼ cup flaked coconut in preheated small, nonstick skillet. Cook, shaking pan often, until coconut is lightly browned, about 4 minutes. Transfer to a small bowl and cool completely.

3. Mash sweet potatoes. Stir in ½ cup walnuts and lime peel. Sprinkle top of mashed sweet potatoes with remaining walnuts and toasted coconut. Serve warm.

Makes 6 to 8 servings

Greek Rice

2 **tablespoons butter**

1¾ **cups uncooked converted long-grain rice**

2 **cans (14 ounces each) low-sodium, fat-free chicken broth**

1 **teaspoon Greek seasoning**

1 **teaspoon ground oregano**

1 **cup pitted kalamata olives, drained and chopped**

¾ **cup chopped roasted red peppers**

Crumbled feta cheese (optional)

Chopped fresh Italian parsley (optional)

Melt butter in large nonstick skillet over medium-high heat. Add rice and sauté 4 minutes or until golden brown. Transfer to **CROCK-POT®** slow cooker. Stir in chicken broth, Greek seasoning, and oregano. Cover and cook on LOW 4 hours or until liquid has all been absorbed and rice is tender. Stir in olives and roasted red peppers and cook 5 minutes more. Garnish with feta and Italian parsley, if desired.

Makes 6 to 8 servings

Busy-Day Rice

2 **cups water**

1 **cup uncooked converted white rice**

2 **tablespoons butter**

1 **tablespoon dried minced onion**

1 **tablespoon dried parsley**

2 **teaspoons chicken bouillon granules**

Dash ground red pepper (optional)

Combine all ingredients in **CROCK-POT®** slow cooker; mix well. Cover; cook on HIGH 2 hours.

Makes 4 servings

Greek Rice

Risotto-Style Peppered Rice

1 **cup uncooked converted
long-grain rice**

1 **medium green bell pepper,
chopped**

1 **medium red bell pepper,
chopped**

1 **cup chopped onion**

$^1/_2$ **teaspoon ground turmeric**

$^1/_8$ **teaspoon ground red
pepper (optional)**

1 **can (14$^1/_2$ ounces) fat-free
chicken broth**

4 **ounces Monterey Jack
cheese with jalapeño
peppers, cubed**

$^1/_2$ **cup milk**

$^1/_4$ **cup ($^1/_2$ stick) butter,
cut into small pieces**

1 **teaspoon salt**

**Tip: Dairy products should
be added at the end of the
cooking time because they
will curdle if cooked in the
CROCK-POT® slow cooker
for a long time.**

1. Place rice, bell peppers, onion, turmeric and ground red pepper, if desired, in **CROCK-POT®** slow cooker. Stir in broth. Cover; cook on LOW 4 to 5 hours or until rice is tender and broth is absorbed.

2. Stir in cheese, milk, butter and salt; fluff rice with fork. Cover; cook on LOW 5 minutes or until cheese melts.

Makes 4 to 6 servings

Macaroni and Cheese

6 cups cooked elbow
  macaroni

2 tablespoons butter

4 cups evaporated milk

6 cups (24 ounces) shredded
  Cheddar cheese

2 teaspoons salt

½ teaspoon black pepper

**Tip: Make this mac 'n'
cheese recipe more fun with
tasty mix-ins: diced green
or red bell pepper, peas, hot
dog slices, chopped tomato,
browned ground beef or
chopped onion.**

Toss macaroni with butter in large bowl. Stir in evaporated milk,
cheese, salt and pepper; place in **CROCK-POT**® slow cooker.
Cover; cook on HIGH 2 to 3 hours.

Makes 6 to 8 servings

No-Fuss Macaroni & Cheese

2 cups (about 8 ounces) uncooked elbow macaroni

4 ounces light pasteurized processed cheese, cubed

1 cup (4 ounces) shredded mild Cheddar cheese

½ teaspoon salt

⅛ teaspoon black pepper

1½ cups fat-free (skim) milk

Combine macaroni, cheeses, salt and pepper in **CROCK-POT®** slow cooker. Pour milk over all. Cover; cook on LOW 2 to 3 hours, stirring after 20 to 30 minutes.

Makes 6 to 8 servings

South-of-the-Border Macaroni & Cheese

5 cups cooked rotini pasta

2 cups (8 ounces) cubed American cheese

1 can (12 ounces) evaporated milk

1 cup (4 ounces) cubed sharp Cheddar cheese

1 can (4 ounces) diced green chiles, drained

2 teaspoons chili powder

2 medium tomatoes, seeded and chopped

5 green onions, sliced

1. Combine pasta, American cheese, evaporated milk, Cheddar cheese, chiles and chili powder in **CROCK-POT®** slow cooker; mix well. Cover; cook on HIGH 2 hours, stirring occasionally.

2. Stir in tomatoes and green onions; continue cooking until heated through.

Makes 4 servings

Vegetable Sides

Tarragon Carrots in White Wine

½ cup chicken broth

½ cup dry white wine

1 tablespoon lemon juice

1 tablespoon minced fresh tarragon

2 teaspoons finely chopped green onions

1½ teaspoons chopped flat-leaf parsley

1 clove garlic, minced

1 teaspoon salt

8 medium carrots, peeled and cut into matchsticks

2 tablespoons melba toast, crushed

2 tablespoons cold water

1. Combine broth, wine, lemon juice, tarragon, onions, parsley, garlic and salt in **CROCK-POT**® slow cooker. Add carrots; stir well to combine. Cover; cook on LOW 2½ to 3 hours or on HIGH 1½ to 2 hours.

2. Turn **CROCK-POT**® slow cooker to LOW. Dissolve toast crumbs in water and add to carrots. Cover; cook 10 minutes longer, or until thickened.

Makes 6 to 8 servings

Braised Sweet and Sour Cabbage and Apples

2 tablespoons unsalted butter

6 cups coarsely shredded red cabbage

1 large sweet apple, peeled, cored and cut into bite-size pieces

3 whole cloves

½ cup raisins

½ cup apple cider

3 tablespoons cider vinegar, divided

2 tablespoons packed dark brown sugar

½ teaspoon salt

¼ teaspoon black pepper

1. Melt butter in very large skillet or shallow pot over medium heat. Add cabbage. Cook and stir 3 minutes until cabbage is glossy. Transfer to **CROCK-POT**® slow cooker.

2. Add apple, cloves, raisins, apple cider, 2 tablespoons vinegar, sugar, salt and pepper. Cover; cook on LOW 2½ to 3 hours.

3. To serve, remove cloves and stir in remaining 1 tablespoon vinegar.

Makes 4 to 6 servings

Mrs. Grady's Beans

½ **pound 90% lean ground beef**

1 **small onion, chopped**

8 **slices bacon, chopped**

1 **can (about 15 ounces) pinto beans, undrained**

1 **can (about 15 ounces) butter beans, rinsed and drained, reserving ¼ cup liquid**

1 **can (about 15 ounces) kidney beans, rinsed and drained**

¼ **cup ketchup**

2 **tablespoons molasses**

½ **teaspoon dry mustard**

½ **cup granulated sugar**

¼ **cup packed brown sugar**

1. Brown ground beef, onion and bacon in medium saucepan over high heat. Stir in beans and liquid; set aside.

2. Combine ketchup, molasses and mustard in medium bowl. Mix in sugars. Stir ketchup mixture into beef mixture; mix well. Transfer to **CROCK-POT**® slow cooker. Cover and cook on LOW 2 to 3 hours or until heated through.

Makes 6 to 8 servings

Manchego Eggplant

4 large eggplants

1 cup flour

2 tablespoons olive oil

1 jar (25½ ounces) roasted garlic flavor pasta sauce, divided

2 tablespoons Italian seasoning, divided

1 cup (4 ounces) grated manchego cheese, divided

1 jar (24 ounces) roasted eggplant flavor marinara, divided

1. Peel eggplants and slice horizontally into ¾-inch-thick pieces. Place flour in shallow bowl. Dredge each slice of eggplant in flour to coat.

2. Heat oil in large skillet over medium-high heat. In batches, lightly brown eggplant on both sides.

3. Pour thin layer of pasta sauce into bottom of **CROCK-POT®** slow cooker. Top with, in order: eggplant slices, Italian seasoning, manchego cheese and roasted eggplant flavor marinara. Repeat layers until all ingredients have been used.

4. Cover and cook on HIGH 2 hours.

Makes 8 to 10 servings

Lemon Dilled Parsnips and Turnips

2 cups chicken broth

1/4 cup chopped scallions

4 tablespoons lemon juice

4 tablespoons dried dill

1 teaspoon minced garlic

4 turnips, peeled and cut into 1/2-inch pieces

3 parsnips, peeled and cut into 1/2-inch pieces

4 tablespoons cornstarch

1/4 cup cold water

1. Combine broth, scallions, lemon juice, dill and garlic in **CROCK-POT®** slow cooker.

2. Add turnips and parsnips; stir. Cover; cook on LOW 3 to 4 hours or on HIGH 1 to 3 hours.

3. Turn **CROCK-POT®** slow cooker to HIGH. Dissolve cornstarch in water. Add to **CROCK-POT®** slow cooker. Stir well to combine. Cover; continue cooking 15 minutes longer or until thickened.

Makes 8 to 10 servings

Oriental Golden Barley with Cashews

2 tablespoons unsalted butter

1 cup hulled barley, sorted

3 cups vegetable broth

1 cup chopped celery

1 green bell pepper, cored, seeded and chopped

1 yellow onion, peeled and minced

1 clove garlic, minced

¼ teaspoon black pepper

¼ cup finely chopped cashews

1. Heat skillet over medium heat until hot. Add butter and barley. Cook and stir about 10 minutes or until barley is slightly browned. Transfer to **CROCK-POT®** slow cooker.

2. Add broth, celery, bell pepper, onion, garlic and black pepper. Stir well to combine. Cover; cook on LOW 4 to 5 hours or on HIGH 2 to 3 hours, or until barley is tender and liquid is absorbed.

3. To serve, garnish with cashews.

Makes 4 servings

Simmered Napa Cabbage with Dried Apricots

4 cups Napa cabbage or
green cabbage, cored,
cleaned and sliced thin
1 cup chopped dried
apricots
¼ cup clover honey
2 tablespoons orange juice
½ cup dry red wine
Salt and black pepper,
to taste
Grated orange peel
(optional)

1. Combine cabbage and apricots in **CROCK-POT**® slow cooker. Toss to mix well.

2. Combine honey and orange juice, mixing until smooth. Drizzle over cabbage. Add wine. Cover; cook on LOW 5 to 6 hours or on HIGH 2 to 3 hours, or until cabbage is tender.

3. Season to taste with salt and pepper. Garnish with orange peel, if desired.

Makes 4 servings

Roasted Summer Squash with Pine Nuts and Romano Cheese

2 tablespoons extra-virgin
olive oil
½ cup chopped yellow onion
1 medium red bell pepper,
cored, seeded and
chopped
1 clove garlic, minced
3 medium zucchini,
cut in ½-inch slices
3 medium summer squash,
cut in ½-inch slices
½ cup chopped pine nuts
⅓ cup grated Romano
cheese
1 teaspoon dried Italian
seasoning
1 teaspoon salt
¼ teaspoon black pepper
1 tablespoon unsalted
butter, cut into small
cubes

1. Heat oil in skillet over medium-high heat until hot. Add onion, bell pepper and garlic. Cook and stir until onion is translucent and soft, about 10 minutes. Transfer to **CROCK-POT**® slow cooker.

2. Add zucchini and summer squash. Toss lightly.

3. Combine pine nuts, cheese, Italian seasoning, salt and black pepper in small bowl. Fold half of cheese mixture into squash. Sprinkle remaining cheese mixture on top. Dot cheese with butter. Cover; cook on LOW 4 to 6 hours.

Makes 6 to 8 servings

**Simmered Napa
Cabbage with
Dried Apricots**

Red Cabbage and Apples

**1 small head red cabbage,
cored and thinly sliced**

**3 medium apples, peeled
and grated**

¾ cup sugar

½ cup red wine vinegar

1 teaspoon ground cloves

**1 cup crisp-cooked and
crumbled bacon (optional)**

**Fresh apple slices
(optional)**

Combine cabbage, apples, sugar, vinegar and cloves in
CROCK-POT® slow cooker. Cover; cook on HIGH 6 hours, stirring
after 3 hours. To serve, sprinkle with bacon and garnish with
apple slices, if desired.

Makes 4 to 6 servings

Scalloped Tomatoes and Corn

1 **can (15 ounces)
cream-style corn**

1 **can (14½ ounces) diced
tomatoes, undrained**

¾ **cup saltine or soda
cracker crumbs**

1 **egg, lightly beaten**

2 **teaspoons sugar**

¾ **teaspoon black pepper**

Chopped fresh tomatoes

Chopped fresh parsley

**Note: Fresh tomatoes are
available all year, although
locally grown summer
tomatoes are superior to all
others. Depending on the
area, tomato season usually
begins in mid-summer and
lasts through September.**

Combine corn, tomatoes with juice, cracker crumbs, egg, sugar
and pepper in **CROCK-POT®** slow cooker; mix well. Cover; cook
on LOW 4 to 6 hours or until done. Sprinkle with tomatoes and
parsley before serving.

Makes 4 to 6 servings

Green Bean Casserole

2 packages (10 ounces each) frozen green beans, thawed

1 can (10¾ ounces) condensed cream of mushroom soup, undiluted

1 tablespoon chopped parsley

1 tablespoon chopped roasted red peppers

1 teaspoon dried sage

½ teaspoon salt

½ teaspoon black pepper

¼ teaspoon ground nutmeg

½ cup toasted slivered almonds

Combine all ingredients except almonds in **CROCK-POT®** slow cooker. Cover; cook on LOW 3 to 4 hours. Sprinkle with almonds before serving.

Makes 4 to 6 servings

Cheesy Corn and Peppers

- **2 pounds frozen corn**
- **2 tablespoons butter, cut into cubes**
- **2 poblano chile peppers, chopped or 1 large green bell pepper and 1 jalapeño, seeded and finely chopped***
- **½ teaspoon ground cumin**
- **1 teaspoon salt**
- **¼ teaspoon coarsely ground black pepper**
- **3 ounces cream cheese, cut into cubes**
- **1 cup (4 ounces) shredded sharp Cheddar cheese**

*Poblano and Jalapeño peppers can sting and irritate the skin; wear rubber gloves when handling peppers and do not touch your eyes. Wash hands after handling.

1. Coat inside of **CROCK-POT**® slow cooker with nonstick cooking spray. Combine all ingredients except cream cheese and Cheddar cheese in **CROCK-POT**® slow cooker. Cover. Cook on HIGH 2 hours.

2. Stir in cheeses. Cover and cook on HIGH 15 minutes more or until cheeses melt.

Makes 8 servings

Asparagus and Cheese

2 cups crushed saltine crackers

1 can (10¾ ounces) condensed cream of asparagus soup, undiluted

1 can (10¾ ounces) condensed cream of chicken soup, undiluted

⅔ cup slivered almonds

4 ounces American cheese, cut into cubes

1 egg

1½ pounds fresh asparagus, trimmed

Combine crackers, soups, almonds, cheese and egg in large bowl; stir well. Pour into **CROCK-POT**® slow cooker. Add asparagus, and stir to coat. Cover; cook on HIGH 3 to 3½ hours or until asparagus is tender. Garnish as desired.

Makes 4 to 6 servings

Tip: Cooking times are guidelines. **CROCK-POT**® slow cookers, just like ovens, cook differently depending on a variety of factors. For example, cooking times will be longer at higher altitudes. You may need to slightly adjust cooking times for your **CROCK-POT**® slow cooker.

Creamy Curried Spinach

3 **packages (10 ounces each) frozen spinach, thawed**

1 **onion, chopped**

4 **teaspoons minced garlic**

2 **tablespoons curry powder**

2 **tablespoons butter, melted**

¼ **cup chicken broth**

¼ **cup heavy cream**

1 **teaspoon lemon juice**

Combine spinach, onion, garlic, curry powder, butter and broth in **CROCK-POT**® slow cooker. Cover; cook on LOW 3 to 4 hours or on HIGH 2 hours or until done. Stir in cream and lemon juice 30 minutes before end of cooking time.

Makes 6 to 8 servings

Braised Beets with Cranberries

2½ **pounds medium beets, peeled and cut in sixths**

½ **cup sweetened dried cranberries**

1 **cup cranberry juice**

2 **tablespoons honey**

2 **tablespoons butter, cut into small pieces**

2 **tablespoons quick-cooking tapioca**

½ **teaspoon salt**

⅓ **cup crumbled blue cheese (optional)**

Orange peel, thinly sliced or grated (optional)

1. Combine beets, cranberries, cranberry juice, honey, butter, tapioca and salt in **CROCK-POT®** slow cooker. Cover and cook on LOW 7 to 8 hours, or until beets are tender.

2. Transfer beets to serving bowl with slotted spoon. Pour half of cooking liquid over beets. Serve warm, at room temperature or chilled. Sprinkle with blue cheese and orange peel, if desired.

Makes 6 to 8 servings

Corn on the Cob with Garlic Herb Butter

½ cup (1 stick) unsalted butter, at room temperature

3 to 4 cloves garlic, minced

2 tablespoons finely minced fresh parsley

4 to 5 ears of corn, husked

Salt and freshly ground black pepper, to taste

1. Thoroughly mix butter, garlic and parsley in small bowl.

2. Place each ear of corn on a piece of aluminum foil and generously spread butter on each ear. Season corn with salt and pepper and tightly seal foil. Place corn in **CROCK-POT**® slow cooker; overlap ears, if necessary. Add enough water to come one-fourth of the way up each ear.

3. Cover; cook on LOW 4 to 5 hours or on HIGH 2 to 2½ hours or until done.

Makes 4 to 5 servings

Cran-Orange Acorn Squash

- **3 small acorn or carnival squash**
- **5 tablespoons instant brown rice**
- **3 tablespoons minced onion**
- **3 tablespoons diced celery**
- **3 tablespoons dried cranberries**
- **Pinch ground or dried sage**
- **1 teaspoon butter, cut into bits**
- **3 tablespoons orange juice**
- **½ cup warm water**

1. Slice off tops of squash and enough of bottoms so squash will sit upright. Scoop out seeds and discard; set squash aside.

2. Combine rice, onion, celery, cranberries and sage in small bowl. Stuff each squash with rice mixture; dot with butter. Pour 1 tablespoon orange juice into each squash over stuffing. Stand squash in **CROCK-POT**® slow cooker. Pour water into bottom of slow cooker.

3. Cover; cook on LOW 2½ hours or until squash are tender.

Makes 6 servings

Baked Beans

- **2 cans (16 ounces each) baked beans**
- **1 cup ketchup**
- **¹⁄₂ cup barbecue sauce**
- **¹⁄₂ cup packed brown sugar**
- **5 slices bacon, chopped**
- **¹⁄₂ green bell pepper, chopped**
- **¹⁄₂ onion, chopped**
- **1¹⁄₂ teaspoons prepared mustard**
- **Fresh parsley (optional)**

Place all ingredients in **CROCK-POT®** slow cooker. Stir well to combine. Cover; cook on LOW 8 to 12 hours or on HIGH 3 to 4 hours. Garnish with fresh parsley, if desired.

Makes 6 to 8 servings

Beverages

Spiced Apple Tea

3 **bags cinnamon herbal tea**

3 **cups boiling water**

2 **cups unsweetened apple juice**

6 **whole cloves**

1 **cinnamon stick**

Place tea bags in **CROCK-POT**® slow cooker. Pour boiling water over tea bags; cover and let stand 10 minutes. Remove and discard tea bags. Add apple juice, cloves and cinnamon stick to **CROCK-POT**® slow cooker. Cover; cook on LOW 2 to 3 hours. Remove and discard cloves and cinnamon stick. Serve warm in mugs.

Makes 4 servings

Warm and Spicy Fruit Punch

4 **cinnamon sticks**

1 **orange, washed**

1 **square (8 inches) double-thickness cheesecloth**

1 **teaspoon whole allspice**

½ **teaspoon whole cloves**

7 **cups water**

1 **can (12 ounces) frozen cran-raspberry juice concentrate, thawed**

1 **can (6 ounces) frozen lemonade concentrate, thawed**

2 **cans (5½ ounces each) apricot nectar**

Tip: To keep punch warm during a party, place your CROCK-POT® slow cooker on the buffet table, and turn the setting to LOW or WARM.

1. Break cinnamon into pieces. Using vegetable peeler, remove strips of orange peel. Squeeze juice from orange; set juice aside.

2. Rinse cheesecloth; squeeze out water. Wrap cinnamon, orange peel, allspice and cloves in cheesecloth. Tie bag securely with cotton string or strip of cheesecloth.

3. Combine reserved orange juice, water, concentrates and apricot nectar in **CROCK-POT®** slow cooker; add spice bag. Cover; cook on LOW 5 to 6 hours. Remove and discard spice bag before serving.

Makes about 14 servings

Hot Mulled Cider

½ gallon apple cider

½ cup packed light brown sugar

1½ teaspoons balsamic or cider vinegar (optional)

1 teaspoon vanilla

1 cinnamon stick

6 whole cloves

½ cup applejack or bourbon (optional)

Combine all ingredients except applejack in **CROCK-POT®** slow cooker. Cover; cook on LOW 5 to 6 hours. Remove and discard cinnamon stick and cloves. Stir in applejack just before serving, if desired. Serve hot in mugs.

Makes 16 servings

Ginger-Lime Martini

2 cups sugar

1 cup water

1 (5-inch) piece fresh ginger, peeled and thinly sliced

3 cups vodka, chilled

2 cups lime juice

Crushed ice

Variation: Homemade Ginger Ale: Pour ½ cup chilled ginger syrup over ice in 16-ounce glass; top off with 1 cup soda water and stir gently to combine.

1. Place sugar, water and ginger into **CROCK-POT®** slow cooker. Cover and cook on LOW 6 to 8 hours or on HIGH 3 to 4 hours.

2. Strain and cool. Refrigerate in airtight container (up to 7 days) until needed.

3. To serve, combine 2 ounces ginger syrup, 3 ounces vodka and 2 ounces lime juice in martini shaker half filled with crushed ice. Shake to combine and then strain into chilled martini glass. Repeat with remaining ingredients.

Makes 8 servings

Hot Mulled Cider

Viennese Coffee

3 cups fresh, hot, strong brewed coffee

3 tablespoons chocolate syrup

1 teaspoon sugar

1/3 cup whipping cream

1/4 cup crème de cacao or Irish cream (optional)

Whipped cream (optional)

Chocolate shavings (optional)

1. Combine coffee, chocolate syrup and sugar in **CROCK-POT**® slow cooker. Cover and cook on LOW 2 to 2½ hours. Stir in whipping cream and crème de cacao, if desired. Cover and cook 30 minutes or until heated through.

2. Ladle coffee into coffee cups. Top with whipped cream and chocolate shavings, if desired.

Makes 4 servings

Infused Mint Mojito

2 cups water

2 cups sugar

2 bunches fresh mint, stems removed

3/4 to 1 cup fresh-squeezed lime juice

1 bottle (750 ml) light rum

2 liters club soda

Fresh mint

1. Place water, sugar and mint in **CROCK-POT**® slow cooker. Cover and cook on HIGH 3½ hours.

2. Strain into large pitcher. Stir in lime juice and rum. Cover and refrigerate until cold.

3. To serve, fill tall glasses halfway with fresh ice. Pour ³/₄ cup mint syrup over ice; top off with club soda to taste. Garnish with additional fresh mint leaves and serve immediately.

Makes 10 to 12 servings

Viennese Coffee

Chai Tea

2 quarts (8 cups) water

8 bags black tea

³/₄ cup sugar*

16 whole cloves

16 whole cardamom seeds,
pods removed (optional)

5 cinnamon sticks

8 slices fresh ginger

1 cup milk

*Chai tea is typically sweet. For
less-sweet tea, reduce sugar to
¹/₂ cup.

1. Combine water, tea, sugar, cloves, cardamom, if desired, cinnamon and ginger in **CROCK-POT**® slow cooker. Cover; cook on HIGH 2 to 2¹/₂ hours.

2. Strain mixture; discard solids. (At this point, tea may be covered and refrigerated up to 3 days.)

3. Stir in milk just before serving. Serve warm or chilled.

Makes 8 to 10 servings

Mocha Supreme

- **2 quarts strong brewed coffee**
- **½ cup instant hot chocolate beverage mix**
- **1 cinnamon stick, broken into halves**
- **1 cup whipping cream**
- **1 tablespoon powdered sugar**

Tip: To whip cream more quickly, chill the beaters and bowl in the freezer for 15 minutes.

1. Place coffee, hot chocolate mix and cinnamon stick halves in **CROCK-POT®** slow cooker; stir. Cover; cook on HIGH 2 to 2½ hours or until hot.

2. Remove and discard cinnamon stick halves.

3. Beat cream in medium bowl with electric mixer on high speed until soft peaks form. Add powdered sugar; beat until stiff peaks form. Ladle hot beverage into mugs; top with whipped cream.

Makes 8 servings

Mucho Mocha Cocoa

1 cup chocolate syrup

⅓ cup instant coffee granules

2 tablespoons sugar (or more to taste)

2 whole cinnamon sticks

1 quart whole milk

1 quart half-and-half

Tip: This is great for a party. If desired, add 1 ounce of rum or whiskey to each serving.

Combine all ingredients in **CROCK-POT®** slow cooker. Stir until well blended. Cover and cook on LOW 3 hours. Serve hot in mugs.

Makes 9 servings

Mulled Cranberry Tea

2 **tea bags**

1 **cup boiling water**

1 **bottle (48 ounces) cranberry juice**

½ **cup dried cranberries (optional)**

⅓ **cup sugar**

1 **large lemon, cut into ¼-inch slices**

4 **cinnamon sticks**

6 **whole cloves**

Additional cinnamon sticks and thin lemon slices (optional)

1. Place tea bags in **CROCK-POT®** slow cooker. Pour boiling water over tea bags; cover and let steep 5 minutes. Remove and discard tea bags.

2. Stir in cranberry juice, cranberries, if desired, sugar, lemon slices, 4 cinnamon sticks and cloves. Cover; cook on LOW 2 to 3 hours or on HIGH 1 to 2 hours.

3. Remove and discard cooked lemon slices, cinnamon sticks and cloves. Serve in warm mug with cinnamon stick or fresh lemon slice, if desired.

Makes 8 servings

Tip: The flavor and aroma of crushed or ground herbs and spices may lessen during a longer cooking time. So, for slow cooking in your **CROCK-POT®** slow cooker, you may use whole herbs and spices. Be sure to taste and adjust your seasonings before serving.

Spiced Citrus Tea

4 tea bags

   Peel of 1 orange

4 cups boiling water

3 tablespoons honey

2 cans (6 ounces each) orange-pineapple juice

3 star anise

3 cinnamon sticks

   Strawberries, raspberries or kiwis (optional)

Place tea bags, orange peel and boiling water in **CROCK-POT®** slow cooker; cover and let steep 10 minutes. Remove and discard tea bags and orange peel. Add remaining ingredients. Cover; cook on LOW 3 hours. Garnish as desired.

Makes 6 servings

Cinnamon Latté

6 cups double-strength brewed coffee*

2 cups half-and-half

1 cup sugar

1 teaspoon vanilla

3 cinnamon sticks, plus additional for garnish

Whipped cream (optional)

*Double the amount of coffee grounds normally used to brew coffee. Or, substitute 8 teaspoons instant coffee dissolved in 6 cups boiling water.

1. Blend coffee, half-and-half, sugar and vanilla in 3- to 4-quart **CROCK-POT**® slow cooker. Add 3 cinnamon sticks. Cover; cook or HIGH 3 hours.

2. Remove cinnamon sticks and discard. Serve latté in tall coffee mugs with dollop of whipped cream and additional cinnamon stick, if desired.

Makes 6 to 8 servings

Desserts

Five-Spice Apple Crisp

3 tablespoons unsalted butter, melted

6 Golden Delicious apples, peeled, cored and cut into ½-inch-thick slices

2 teaspoons fresh lemon juice

¼ cup packed light brown sugar

¾ teaspoon five-spice powder or ½ teaspoon ground cinnamon and ¼ teaspoon ground allspice

1 cup coarsely crushed Chinese-style almond cookies or almond biscotti

Sweetened whipped cream (optional)

1. Brush 4½-quart **CROCK-POT®** slow cooker with melted butter. Add apples and lemon juice and toss to combine. Sprinkle with brown sugar and five-spice powder and toss again.

2. Cover; cook for 3½ hours on LOW or until apples are tender. Sprinkle cookies over apples. Spoon into bowls and serve warm, garnished with whipped cream, if desired.

Makes 4 servings

Sticky Caramel Pumpkin Cake

2 cups all-purpose flour

2 teaspoons baking powder

1 teaspoon baking soda

½ teaspoon pumpkin pie spice or ground cinnamon

½ teaspoon salt

1 cup (2 sticks) unsalted butter, at room temperature

1⅓ cups sugar

4 eggs, at room temperature

1 can (15 ounces) solid-pack pumpkin

1 jar (16 ounces) caramel sauce or caramel ice cream topping

Vanilla ice cream (optional)

1. Coat 4½-quart **CROCK-POT**® slow cooker with nonstick cooking spray.

2. Whisk together flour, baking powder, baking soda, pumpkin pie spice and salt in large bowl. Beat butter and sugar in separate bowl with electric mixer on high speed until light, about 3 minutes. Add eggs one at a time, beating with mixer to incorporate each egg before adding another. Beat in pumpkin. With mixer running on low speed, carefully add flour mixture and beat until smooth. Spread evenly in cooker. Cover; cook on HIGH 2 to 2½ hours or until toothpick inserted in center of cake comes out clean. Drizzle ½ cup caramel sauce over cake. Spoon into bowls and serve warm with ice cream, if desired, and drizzle with additional caramel sauce.

Makes 8 servings

Mexican Chocolate Bread Pudding

1½ **cups light cream**

4 **ounces unsweetened chocolate, coarsely chopped**

2 **eggs, beaten**

½ **cup sugar**

¾ **teaspoon ground cinnamon**

½ **teaspoon ground allspice**

1 **teaspoon vanilla**

⅛ **teaspoon salt**

½ **cup currants**

3 **cups Hawaiian-style sweet bread, challah or rich egg bread, cut into ½-inch cubes**

Whipped cream (optional)

Chopped macadamia nuts (optional)

1. Heat cream in large saucepan. Add chocolate and stir until chocolate melts.

2. Combine eggs, sugar, cinnamon, allspice, vanilla and salt in medium bowl. Stir in currants. Add to chocolate mixture. Stir well to combine. Pour into **CROCK-POT**® slow cooker.

3. Gently fold in bread cubes using plastic spatula. Cover; cook on HIGH 3 to 4 hours or until a knife inserted near center comes out clean.

4. Serve warm or chilled. If desired, top with generous dollop of whipped cream and sprinkling of nuts.

Makes 6 to 8 servings

Orange Soufflé

6 **tablespoons unsalted butter, softened, divided**

1¼ **cups sugar, divided**

Grated peel of 1 orange

6 **tablespoons all-purpose flour**

½ **cup milk**

8 **egg yolks**

6 **tablespoons orange-flavored liqueur**

1 **tablespoon vanilla**

10 **egg whites**

1 **teaspoon salt**

1. Evenly coat interior of **CROCK-POT®** slow cooker with 2 tablespoons softened butter. Pour in ⅓ cup sugar; turn to evenly coat bottom and sides of **CROCK-POT®** slow cooker.

2. Process ⅔ cup sugar and orange peel in food processor until orange peel is evenly ground and well combined.

3. Whisk flour and milk together in medium saucepan. Beat in sugar and orange peel. Cook over medium heat, stirring gently until beginning to thicken. Continue cooking, whisking constantly, until boiling. Cook 30 seconds more then remove from heat. Let cool slightly then beat in egg yolks one at a time.

4. Add 4 tablespoons butter, orange liqueur and vanilla to the mixture and let stand at room temperature 20 minutes to cool.

5. Beat egg whites in clean, dry bowl until foamy. Add salt and beat to soft peaks. Sprinkle in remaining ¼ cup sugar and beat to stiff peaks.

6. Fold one-quarter of beaten egg whites into cooled batter. Fold in remaining egg whites then gently transfer to prepared **CROCK-POT®** slow cooker. Cover and cook on HIGH 1 hour or until soufflé is fully set. Serve immediately.

Makes 10 servings

Triple Chocolate Fantasy

2 **pounds white almond bark, broken into pieces**

1 **bar (4 ounces) sweetened chocolate, broken into pieces***

1 **package (12 ounces) semisweet chocolate chips**

3 **cups lightly toasted, coarsely chopped pecans****

*Use your favorite high-quality chocolate candy bar.

**To toast pecans, spread in single layer on baking sheet. Bake in preheated 350°F oven 8 to 10 minutes or until golden brown, stirring frequently.

Variations: Here are a few ideas for other imaginative items to add in along with or instead of pecans: raisins, crushed peppermint candy, candy-coated baking bits, crushed toffee, peanuts or pistachios, chopped gum drops, chopped dried fruit, candied cherries, chopped marshmallows or sweetened coconut.

1. Place bark, sweetened chocolate and chocolate chips in **CROCK-POT**® slow cooker. Cover; cook on HIGH 1 hour. Do not stir.

2. Turn **CROCK-POT**® slow cooker to LOW. Continue cooking 1 hour, stirring every 15 minutes. Stir in nuts.

3. Drop mixture by tablespoonfuls onto baking sheet covered with waxed paper; let cool. Store in tightly covered container.

Makes 36 pieces

Blueberry Cobbler

¾ **cup biscuit mix**

½ **cup packed brown sugar**

⅓ **cup granulated sugar**

2 **large eggs**

1 **teaspoon vanilla**

½ **teaspoon almond extract**

1 **can (5 ounces) evaporated milk**

2 **teaspoons melted butter**

3 **cups fresh or frozen blueberries**

Vanilla ice cream

1. Spray inside of **CROCK-POT**® slow cooker with nonstick cooking spray. In large bowl, combine biscuit mix and sugars. Add eggs, vanilla and almond extract. Stir to combine. Add evaporated milk and butter. Stir until fully combined.

2. Pour about one-fourth batter into prepared **CROCK-POT**® slow cooker. Place blueberries on top. Pour remaining batter over blueberries. Cover and cook on LOW 5 to 6 hours. Serve warm with ice cream.

Makes 4 to 6 servings

Peanut Fudge Pudding Cake

1 cup all-purpose flour

1 cup sugar, divided

1½ teaspoons baking powder

⅔ cup milk

2 tablespoons vegetable oil

1 teaspoon vanilla

½ cup peanut butter

¼ cup unsweetened cocoa powder

1 cup boiling water

Chopped peanuts (optional)

Vanilla ice cream (optional)

Tip: Because this recipe makes its own fudge topping, be sure to spoon some of it from the bottom of the CROCK-POT® slow cooker when serving, or invert the cake for a luscious chocolatey finish.

1. Coat 4½-quart **CROCK-POT®** slow cooker with nonstick cooking spray or butter. Combine flour, ½ cup sugar and baking powder in medium bowl. Add milk, oil, vanilla and peanut butter. Mix until well blended. Pour batter into **CROCK-POT®** slow cooker.

2. Combine remaining ½ cup sugar and cocoa in small bowl. Stir in water. Pour into prepared **CROCK-POT®** slow cooker. Do not stir.

3. Cover; cook on HIGH 1¼ to 1½ hours or until toothpick inserted into center comes out clean. Allow cake to rest 10 minutes, then scoop into serving dishes or invert onto serving platter. Serve warm with chopped peanuts and ice cream, if desired.

Makes 4 servings

Chocolate Malt Pudding Cake

2 tablespoons unsalted butter

1 cup all-purpose flour

$^1/_2$ cup packed brown sugar

2 tablespoons unsweetened cocoa powder

$1^1/_2$ teaspoons baking powder

$^1/_2$ cup milk

2 tablespoons vegetable oil

$^1/_2$ teaspoon almond extract

$^1/_2$ cup coarsely chopped malted milk balls

$^1/_2$ cup semisweet chocolate chips

$^3/_4$ cup granulated sugar

$^1/_4$ cup malted milk powder

2 cups boiling water

4 ounces cream cheese, cubed, at room temperature

$^1/_4$ cup sliced almonds (optional)

Vanilla ice cream (optional)

1. Generously butter $4^1/_2$-quart **CROCK-POT**® slow cooker. Combine flour, brown sugar, cocoa powder and baking powder in medium bowl. Add milk, oil and almond extract. Stir until smooth.

2. Stir in malted milk balls and chocolate chips. Spread batter evenly in bottom of **CROCK-POT**® slow cooker.

3. Combine granulated sugar and malted milk powder in medium bowl. Mix boiling water and cream cheese in another bowl. Stir into malted milk mixture. Pour evenly over batter in **CROCK-POT**® slow cooker. Do not stir. Cover; cook on HIGH 2 to $2^1/_2$ hours or until toothpick inserted in center comes out clean.

4. Let stand, uncovered, 30 minutes. Spoon into dessert dishes. Garnish with almonds and serve with ice cream, if desired.

Makes 6 to 8 servings

Hot Fudge Cake

1³⁄₄ **cups packed light brown sugar, divided**

2 **cups all-purpose flour**

1⁄₄ **cup plus 3 tablespoons unsweetened cocoa powder, divided, plus additional for dusting (optional)**

2 **teaspoons baking powder**

1 **teaspoon salt**

1 **cup milk**

4 **tablespoons (1⁄2 stick) butter, melted**

1 **teaspoon vanilla**

3¹⁄₂ **cups boiling water**

1. Coat 4¹⁄₂-quart **CROCK-POT®** slow cooker with nonstick cooking spray or butter. Mix 1 cup sugar, flour, 3 tablespoons cocoa powder, baking powder and salt in medium bowl. Stir in milk, butter and vanilla. Mix until well blended. Pour into **CROCK-POT®** slow cooker.

2. Blend remaining ³⁄₄ cup sugar and ¹⁄₄ cup cocoa powder in small bowl. Sprinkle evenly over mixture in **CROCK-POT®** slow cooker. Pour in boiling water. Do not stir.

3. Cover; cook on HIGH 1¹⁄₄ to 1¹⁄₂ hours or until toothpick inserted into center comes out clean. Allow cake to rest 10 minutes, then invert onto serving platter or scoop into serving dishes. Serve warm; dust with cocoa powder, if desired.

Makes 6 to 8 servings

Bittersweet Chocolate-Espresso Crème Brûlée

½ **cup chopped bittersweet chocolate**

5 **egg yolks**

1¾ **cups heavy cream**

¼ **cup espresso**

½ **cup granulated sugar**

¼ **cup Demerara or raw sugar**

1. Arrange 5 (6-ounce) ramekins or custard cups inside **CROCK-POT®** slow cooker. Pour enough water to come halfway up sides of ramekins (taking care to keep water out of ramekins). Divide chocolate among ramekins.

2. Whisk egg yolks briefly; set aside. Heat cream, espresso and granulated sugar in small saucepan over medium heat, stirring constantly, until mixture begins to boil. Pour hot cream in thin, steady stream into egg yolks, whisking constantly. Pour through fine mesh strainer into clean bowl.

3. Ladle into prepared ramekins in bottom of **CROCK-POT®** slow cooker. Cover and cook on HIGH 1 to 2 hours or until custard is set around edges but still soft in centers. Carefully remove and cool to room temperature, then cover and refrigerate until serving.

4. Spread tops of custards with Demerara sugar just before serving; melt with kitchen torch. Serve immediately.

Makes 5 servings

S'Mores Fondue

1 **pound milk chocolate, chopped**

2 **jars (7 ounces each) marshmallow créme**

²/₃ **cup half-and-half**

2 **teaspoons vanilla**

4 **bananas**

1 **cup mini marshmallows**

24 **graham crackers**

24 **strawberries**

1. Combine chocolate, marshmallow créme, half-and-half and vanilla in **CROCK-POT®** slow cooker. Cover and cook on LOW 1½ to 3 hours, stirring after 1 hour.

2. Meanwhile, peel bananas and cut into ½-inch slices. Sprinkle top of fondue dip with mini marshmallows and serve with banana slices, graham crackers and strawberries.

Makes 8 to 12 servings

Caramel and Apple Pound Cake

4 medium baking apples, cored, peeled and cut into wedges

½ cup apple juice

½ pound caramels, unwrapped

¼ cup creamy peanut butter

1½ teaspoons vanilla

½ teaspoon ground cinnamon

⅛ teaspoon ground cardamom

1 prepared pound cake, sliced

1. Coat inside of **CROCK-POT**® slow cooker with nonstick cooking spray. Layer apples, apple juice and caramels in **CROCK-POT**® slow cooker.

2. Mix together peanut butter, vanilla, cinnamon and cardamom in small bowl. Drop by teaspoons onto apples. Cover; cook on LOW 6 to 8 hours or on HIGH 3 to 4 hours.

3. Stir thoroughly, and cook 1 hour longer. To serve, spoon warm over cake slices.

Makes 6 to 8 servings

Baked Ginger Apples

4 large Red Delicious apples

½ cup (1 stick) unsalted butter, melted

⅓ cup chopped macadamia nuts

¼ cup chopped dried apricots

2 tablespoons finely chopped crystallized ginger

1 tablespoon dark brown sugar

¾ cup brandy

½ cup vanilla pudding and pie filling mix

2 cups heavy cream

Tip: Don't worry about using spirits or liqueurs in slow-cooked dessert recipes. The gentle heat causes the alcohol content to cook away, leaving only the delicious flavor behind.

1. Slice tops off apples; remove cores. Combine butter, nuts, apricots, ginger and brown sugar in medium bowl. Fill apples with nut mixture. Transfer to **CROCK-POT®** slow cooker. Pour brandy over apples. Cover; cook on LOW 4 hours or on HIGH 2 hours.

2. Gently remove apples from **CROCK-POT®** slow cooker with slotted spoon; cover with foil to keep warm.

3. Combine pudding mix and cream in small bowl. Add to cooking liquid in **CROCK-POT®** slow cooker; mix well. Cover; cook on HIGH 30 minutes. Stir until smooth. Return apples to **CROCK-POT®** slow cooker; keep warm until ready to serve with warm cream sauce.

Makes 4 servings

Cinn-Sational Swirl Cake

1 box (21½ ounces) cinnamon swirl cake mix

1 package (4-serving size) instant French vanilla pudding and pie filling mix

1 cup sour cream

1 cup cinnamon-flavored baking chips

1 cup water

¾ cup vegetable oil

Cinnamon ice cream (optional)

1. Coat 4½-quart **CROCK-POT®** slow cooker with nonstick cooking spray. Set cinnamon swirl mix packet aside. Mix remaining cake mix with French vanilla pudding and pie filling mix. Place in **CROCK-POT®** slow cooker.

2. Add sour cream, cinnamon chips, water and oil; stir well to combine. Batter will be slightly lumpy. Add reserved cinnamon swirl mix, slowly swirling through batter with knife. Cover; cook on LOW 3 to 4 hours or on HIGH 1½ to 1¾ hours or until toothpick inserted into center of cake comes out clean.

3. Serve warm with cinnamon ice cream, if desired.

Makes 10 to 12 servings

Streusel Pound Cake

1 **package (16 ounces) pound cake mix, plus ingredients to prepare mix**

¼ **cup packed light brown sugar**

1 **tablespoon all-purpose flour**

¼ **cup chopped nuts**

1 **teaspoon ground cinnamon**

Strawberries, blueberries, raspberries and/or powdered sugar (optional)

Coat 4½-quart **CROCK-POT®** slow cooker with nonstick cooking spray. Prepare cake mix according to package directions; stir in brown sugar, flour, nuts and cinnamon. Pour batter into **CROCK-POT®** slow cooker. Cover; cook on HIGH 1½ to 1¾ hours or until toothpick inserted into center of cake comes out clean. Serve with berries and powdered sugar, if desired.

Makes 6 to 8 servings

Fresh Berry Compote

2 cups fresh blueberries

4 cups fresh sliced strawberries

2 tablespoons orange juice

½ to ¾ cup sugar

4 slices (½ × 1½ inches) lemon peel with no white pith

1 cinnamon stick or ½ teaspoon ground cinnamon

Tip: To turn this compote into a fresh-fruit topping for cake, ice cream, waffles or pancakes, carefully spoon out fruit, leaving cooking liquid in CROCK-POT® slow cooker. Blend 1 to 2 tablespoons cornstarch with ¼ cup cold water until smooth. Add to cooking liquid and cook on HIGH until thickened. Return fruit to sauce and blend in gently.

1. Place blueberries in **CROCK-POT®** slow cooker. Cover; cook on HIGH 45 minutes until blueberries begin to soften.

2. Add strawberries, orange juice, ½ cup sugar, lemon peel and cinnamon stick. Stir to blend. Cover; cook on HIGH 1 to 1½ hours or until berries soften and sugar dissolves. Check for sweetness and add more sugar if necessary, cooking until added sugar dissolves.

3. Remove insert from **CROCK-POT®** slow cooker to heatproof surface and let cool. Serve compote warm or chilled.

Makes 4 servings

Recipe Index

Braised Chipotle Beef (page 82)

Recipe Index

**Viennese Coffee
(page 278)**

Cream Cheese Chicken with Broccoli (page 118)

Recipe Index

Braised Sweet and Sour Cabbage and Apples (page 250)

N-O

P

Pork

Mrs. Grady's Beans (page 252)

Ham with Fruited Bourbon Sauce (page 179)

Recipe Index

Vegetable Jollof Rice *(page 210)*

Metric Chart

VOLUME MEASUREMENTS (dry)

¹/₈ teaspoon = 0.5 mL
¹/₄ teaspoon = 1 mL
¹/₂ teaspoon = 2 mL
³/₄ teaspoon = 4 mL
1 teaspoon = 5 mL
1 tablespoon = 15 mL
2 tablespoons = 30 mL
¹/₄ cup = 60 mL
¹/₃ cup = 75 mL
¹/₂ cup = 125 mL
²/₃ cup = 150 mL
³/₄ cup = 175 mL
1 cup = 250 mL
2 cups = 1 pint = 500 mL
3 cups = 750 mL
4 cups = 1 quart = 1 L

VOLUME MEASUREMENTS (fluid)

1 fluid ounce (2 tablespoons) = 30 mL
4 fluid ounces (¹/₂ cup) = 125 mL
8 fluid ounces (1 cup) = 250 mL
12 fluid ounces (1¹/₂ cups) = 375 mL
16 fluid ounces (2 cups) = 500 mL

WEIGHTS (mass)

¹/₂ ounce = 15 g
1 ounce = 30 g
3 ounces = 90 g
4 ounces = 120 g
8 ounces = 225 g
10 ounces = 285 g
12 ounces = 360 g
16 ounces = 1 pound = 450 g

DIMENSIONS

¹/₁₆ inch = 2 mm
¹/₈ inch = 3 mm
¹/₄ inch = 6 mm
¹/₂ inch = 1.5 cm
³/₄ inch = 2 cm
1 inch = 2.5 cm

OVEN TEMPERATURES

250°F = 120°C
275°F = 140°C
300°F = 150°C
325°F = 160°C
350°F = 180°C
375°F = 190°C
400°F = 200°C
425°F = 220°C
450°F = 230°C

BAKING PAN AND DISH EQUIVALENTS

Utensil	Size in Inches	Size in Centimeters	Volume	Metric Volume
Baking or Cake Pan (square or rectangular)	8×8×2	20×20×5	8 cups	2 L
	9×9×2	23×23×5	10 cups	2.5 L
	13×9×2	33×23×5	12 cups	3 L
Loaf Pan	8½×4½×2½	21×11×6	6 cups	1.5 L
	9×9×3	23×13×7	8 cups	2 L
Round Layer Cake Pan	8×1½	20×4	4 cups	1 L
	9×1½	23×4	5 cups	1.25 L
Pie Plate	8×1½	20×4	4 cups	1 L
	9×1½	23×4	5 cups	1.25 L
Baking Dish or Casserole			1 quart/4 cups	1 L
			1½ quart/6 cups	1.5 L
			2 quart/8 cups	2 L
			3 quart/12 cups	3 L